BUILDING COLLABORATIVE LEARNING ENVIRONMENTS: THE EFFECTS OF TRUST AND ITS RELATIONSHIP TO LEARNING IN THE 3-D VIRTUAL EDUCATION ENVIRONMENT OF SECOND LIFE

By

CHRISTINA B. STEELE

BS University of Utah, 1996

MS Touro University International, 2006

MBA Touro University International, 2007

A dissertation submitted in partial fulfillment of the requirements

for the degree of Doctor of Computer Science: Emerging Media

to the faculty of the Institute of Advanced Studies

of Colorado Technical University

Colorado Springs, Colorado

June 12, 2013

ISBN-13: 978-0615861265

ISBN-10: 0615861261

Twitter: https://twitter.com/steeleshark

Blog: christinasteele.blogspot.com/

LinkedIn: www.linkedin.com/in/drchristinasteele/

DISSERTATION IS APPROVED BY:

Anne-Marie Armstrong, PhD, Chair

Cynthia M. Calongne, DCS

Andrew Stricker, PhD

DEDICATION

This dissertation is dedicated to my amazing pool boy. Tom, without your endless patience, understanding, inspiration and support, this endeavor would not have been possible.

ACKNOWLEDGMENTS

It is with deep gratitude that I thank my dissertation committee. Dr. Anne-Marie Armstrong, I could not have asked for a better mentor. Your guidance, advice and support have helped me to realize this dream. Dr. Cynthia "Lyr" Calongne, it was your passion and enthusiasm for SL which rubbed off on me, and helped me to realize the incredible potential of this emerging media. Dr. Andy Stricker, thank you for teaching me to see the "art of the possible", where our imagination is truly the only limit. All of you, and your wisdom, guidance, feedback, and brainstorming sessions helped me to stay focused and on-track. I am going to miss all of your insightful comments, witty ideas and enriching enthusiasm. I would also like to thank Dr. Boje for his introduction to storytelling as a qualitative method. Thank you to Kel Pero, your editorial expertise and focus on all the important details made this a manuscript that I am very proud of. Lastly, the deepest thanks goes to my husband for your tenacious support and engaging discussions on my academic desires. Thank you for helping me to stay focused on the fact that "the best dissertation is a DONE dissertation". I am looking forward to moving on to my next journey.

"Those who trust us educate us" ~ TS Eliot

Abstract

This dissertation, helps to provide a foundational understanding of trust in virtual worlds by exploring, in particular, the potential learning benefits enabled by the educator building trust in these unique environments. The research methodology is based on Creswell's qualitative design, and Boje's storytelling construct is used to explore trust in virtual environments used for learning. An extensive review of published research led to the discovery of learning affordances such as the facilitation of tasks to enhance trust and improve the contextualization of learning, compared to tasks made possible by 2-D alternatives. This study addresses how the facilitator creates trust and an effective collaborative learning group. This study concludes that a narrative is a web of living stories that binds learning communities together. The current study also contends that the continued investment in 3-D virtual worlds for educational purposes should be considered, contingent upon investigation into the interpersonal relationships, which are present in virtual worlds and their use for learning. 3-D immersive virtual worlds as exemplified by Second Life are used for entertainment, business, and education purposes, and to facilitate a wide variety of activities online. Meanwhile, researchers also see the significant impact of such environments on distance learning. However, most research in this area has focused on the use of virtual worlds as a tool for enhancing engagement but there is a lack of research on the how trust affects learning in the virtual world. Managing teams of students and faculty in this context requires a deeper understanding of people, processes, technology, and the role of trust in virtual worlds compared to face-to-face interactions.

Keywords: Second Life, virtual worlds, trust, education, immersive, learning, storytelling

Contents

Chapter I: Introduction

The virtual world is an emerging medium that allows for immersive communication. Whether we are videoconferencing with a student across the ocean or e-mailing a colleague sitting in the next cubicle, we communicate differently now than in earlier eras because of technology. Virtual environments are among these revolutionizing technologies, and regularly facilitate communication between people, whether on the road, at home, at customer sites, or even on opposite sides of the globe. This type of communication technology allows for faster decision-making of leaders and reduced costs in infrastructures, yet the lack of face-to-face interaction can have negative repercussions. For instance, the lack of an in-person relationship has implications for trust, cooperation, and creativity (Roger & Johnson, 1994; Kanawattanachai & Yoo, 2002; Thompson & Nadler, 2002). The issue of trust, in particular, is critical in the context of virtual environments and teams. Since these teams exist in conditions of ambiguity and complexity, coordinated action is more effective if trust is present among team members (Peters & Manz, 2007). In these virtual environments, the development of relationships is different from the norm, and often complicated by the social dimensions of working together virtually, which is not the same experience as when teams are co-located or face-to-face (Greenberg, et al., 2007; D. Owens, 2012).

With the recent global economic meltdown, there have been forced budget cuts and a drive for economic efficiencies. Several institutions have turned to emerging media formats, such as internet-based distance learning, realize these efficiencies, support education initiatives, and the expectation is that interest in these formats will continue to grow (Allen & Seaman, 2007). Additionally, academia is faced with the challenge of remaining relevant and delivering quality education despite fiscal constraints and fewer resources. Educators are seeking to make use of emerging media to improve curricula, enable efficiencies, and offer cutting-edge learning environments. With increases in demand for online education, it is necessary to understand the emergent Web-enabled media that can contribute to learning (Guru & Nah, 2001).

One of the most relevant forms of emerging media used to offer distance-learning opportunities is the immersive virtual world. The virtual world provides a place where people can gather together as *avatars*, pictorial representations of users, to interact with each other in computer-generated spaces online. There are a number of different virtual environments, ranging from popular social media sites such as Facebook to three-dimensional (3-D) immersive systems such as Second Life, in which populations of users socialize in a persistent virtual world (Hayes, 2006). As educators move into this environment, challenges arise from the lack of face-to-face interaction. There is evidence in the literature that one of the ways this challenge can be addressed is through the use of virtual teams (DeJong & Elfring, 2010). It is thus increasingly important to understand the significance of dynamics in virtual learning environments as educators are faced with the challenges of learning how their students interact as members of a virtual team. It is also necessary to have an understanding of the construct of trust in these environments, and the impact of trust on learning. This dissertation sought to bring together research on how trust affects the way people interact in virtual environments, and the consequences for education; specifically, this work addressed the gap in the literature concerning how trust supports learning in 3-D virtual environments. The qualitative study conducted here offers a framework for understanding the technology of the virtual world and its future implications for educators. The virtual environment for this study was the virtual world of Second Life.

Background

Not long ago, virtual worlds were barely a blip on the radar of popular consciousness. Every day, a new communication technology hits the market, and we are seeing a growing dependency on constant connection through mobile devices. Looking around, it is easy to see how emerging media is affecting every corner of our lives (Ball State University, 2011).

In a quest for further knowledge, researchers conduct reviews to evaluate the current state of an area within a discipline and the documented literature on the topic. One topic is virtual worlds and virtual environments as a whole. An aspect that researchers recommend for further exploration is the role of trust in virtual environments (Zornoza, Orengo, & Peñarroja, 2009) and the use of virtual teams for learning (Martins, Gilson, & Maynard, 2004). One of the greatest challenges of learning with the virtual team construct is building and sustaining trust, together with interpersonal processes and shared understandings (Gibson & Manuel, 2003; Jarvenpaa & Leidner, 1999;

Maznevski & Chudoba, 2000). The studies within the discipline are mainly quantitative, and support the conclusion that the greater the trust the virtual team members' exhibit, the more effective the group outcomes will be. With this as a starting premise, the investigator examined trust in more detail, within the context of learning in virtual environments. This will be a significant platform to study as an emerging medium, since, according to the Strategy Analytics' report called "Virtual Worlds Market Forecast 2009-2015" (Gilbert, 2009), worldwide revenue from the sale of virtual goods is forecast to reach $17 billion by 2015. Social networking sites are among those virtual environments that have seen significant increases in online activity (Davis, et al. 2009). Facebook, has grown to more than 250 million users worldwide, with nearly half of them logging in at least once per day (Facebook.com, 2010). Even at the height of the recent global economic depression, the economic growth of Second Life was an amazing 94 percent in 2008 and an additional 65 percent in 2009, with Second Life reporting an economy of $567 million in US dollars in 2009 (Linden Research, Inc., 2010).

Purpose of this Study

This study aims to contribute to a better understanding of the function of trust in virtual environments, and to build a rich, detailed description of the role of virtual environments in education. This study examined the personal stories of educators, including the experiences that led them to integrate trust into their virtual classroom environments and to create collaborative learning teams or communities. Educators told stories that reflected back on their experiences with the ways in which emerging media was used in educational contexts to build trust in virtual worlds. The main goal of this study was thus to explore the ways in which trust is perceived in virtual environments as a means to examine further the function of trust in virtual education. This study serves as a foundation for further exploration of how virtual worlds are used for learning, and this dissertation meets a need in the current literature to bridge the gap between studies of face-to-face contexts and those of the unique features of 3-D virtual worlds.

Research Question. Leedy and Ormrod (2001) stated clearly that a research question would allow the investigator to obtain good research. While several questions are posed in this study to explore the topic, the focus of this dissertation is guided by the question: *What are the effects of trust and its relationship to learning in 3-D virtual educational environments?*

Goals and Need for this Study. While the concept of trust and how educators can create it has been studied over time with increasing precision by a variety of scholars, there is a need to explore the role educators play in using emerging media effectively to facilitate trust in virtual environments, making this a nascent theory (Edmondson & McManus, 2007). Since there exists remarkably little research on the roles of trust and emerging media within the virtual environment, this research is considered an outlier, meaning it exists outside the "mean tendency" (Edmondson & McManus, 2007, p. 1168). My research questions in this study stem from how trust is built and perceived; how trust as a component of social capital is created in the virtual environment; how educators use emerging media; and how virtual environments change the construct of trust in virtual teams.

The influence of interpersonal factors must be considered in any evaluation of the current research on relationships and group outcomes in virtual environments. The link between processes and environment called for open-ended questions, interviews, observations, and analysis and assessment to see if new patterns emerge, suggesting further work or a new theory (Edmondson & McManus, 2007). Additionally, this study evaluated the educator and student relationships to identify whether any patterns seen in studies of the physical classroom can apply to virtual classrooms. The investigator used narrative research (storytelling) to explore the views of the participants (attitudinal/psychological factors regarding trust in virtual interaction), achieving what some believe to be the best methodological fit for this type of research (Edmondson & McManus, 2007).

This research study recognized that virtual worlds are increasing in popularity and have garnered significant attention from a wide spectrum of the public, from corporate organizations to scholars in diverse interdisciplinary areas. According to Mennecke et al. (2008), "hundreds of publicly accessible virtual worlds exist and firms like Forterra Systems build and manage countless numbers of private virtual worlds used for corporate or military applications" (p. 372). Several scholars have explored the use of this technology in both the corporate and academic arenas (Franceschi, Lee, Zanakis, & Hinds, 2009; Haenlein & Kaplan, 2009; Jin & Lee, 2010; Schultze &

Orlikowski, 2010). However, the aspect of trust as a component of social capital in virtual worlds remains an area that requires further exploration (Hoffmann & Novak, 2009; Jin & Lee, 2010). Investigating how educators can create trust in the virtual world environment is thus worthwhile. As stated, the purpose of this research study was to examine the stories of educators who have experience in building trust in the virtual classroom.

Chapter two of this dissertation contains a detailed literature review, which explores the ways in which social capital and trust are perceived in virtual teams, virtual worlds, and virtual classrooms, while more closely relating trust to the roles emerging media are playing in education and the virtual environment. Through an extensive literature review, this chapter examined experiences with virtual environments, social capital, trust, and emerging media to assess the current state of research in this emerging field and to identify the need for further analysis. Then the research study sought to compare the similarities and differences among educators' stories, using qualitative narrative techniques. The study consisted of a detailed narrative analysis, which revealed the essential themes and meanings within the group (Ryan & Bernard, 2000). The investigator then explored how this work can serve as a foundation for future research.

This research supports the popular conception of contemporary students as being "wired" to learn (Ripamonti, 2009) and emphasizes the importance of educators keeping pace with their learners. In the past decade, the technology revolution has pushed educational institutions to keep abreast of the latest technologies to stay relevant; as a result, many higher education institutions are now equipped to deal with the demand for high-tech applications for learning. Today, the question with which educators struggle the most is not whether computers belong in the classroom, but rather how we can use them most effectively. Frequently, however, educators are ill-equipped to deal with emerging technologies; the result is that, even with access to the latest tools, universities are struggling with how best to implement innovative technologies in the classroom. To meet evolving student needs, there is a requirement to find cutting-edge ways to facilitate learning. Studies have consistently shown that when educators teach with interactive tools, today's "wired" students learn better, and their test scores improve because interactive content sparks interest, engages attention, and fosters learning (Ripamonti, 2009; Kidd & Chen, 2009).

One example of these interactive tools is virtual worlds, such as Second Life. Colorado Technical University, a multi-campus university based in Colorado Springs, Colorado is meeting the demand for interactive high-tech learning by offering classes in Second Life. Many large universities are using this technology to offer the level of interactivity needed to engage students with cutting-edge multimedia.

Virtual worlds are drawing in an astounding number of people (Book, 2004; Hayes, 2006). A *virtual world* can be described as a computer-based, simulated 3-D environment in which persistent networks of people share a social space (Bell, 2008; Book, 2004; Candle, 1965). Virtual worlds are immersive and have a social media component, allowing for user-created content and a sense of sharing presence with others in the same time and place (Cooper, 2009). In an educational context, the distinguishing feature of virtual worlds is that this level of immersive presence moves beyond the traditional formats of distance learning to become a tool that is used in formal instruction and informal education in the form of knowledge sharing (Ondrejka, 2008).

Virtual worlds are an emerging frontier with critical implications for higher education. Many institutions have already begun to use this medium, because it allows students to work virtually in teams in any geographic area at any time. This qualitative research study explored the question of how educators use emerging media such as that used in virtual worlds to build trust in virtual learning environments.

Problem Statement. Although there has been a significant increase in the use and significance of virtual worlds in education contexts, little is still known about their strengths and limitations as learning environments (Hayes, 2006; Cooper, 2009). Additionally, these environments, when compared to other educational media, are still new and complex. Due to the interdisciplinary nature of the empirical studies on this subject, most virtual team research comes from the management field, while virtual worlds are found in the IT and computer field, virtual education is found in the academic field. Thus, very little research exists combining these topics on virtual teams in virtual education settings such as Second Life. Therefore, the problem statement resolved is: *there is a need for exploration of the ways in which trust is perceived and built in virtual environments as a means to examine further the function of trust in education*. The investigator sought to describe the role educators play in establishing trust as a component of social capital in the virtual environment, and to build a rich, detailed description of how trust can be facilitated in virtual settings. Earlier studies have also demonstrated that social capital and, specifically, trust are critical parts of the learning environment (Davis et al., 2009; Schultze & Orlikowski, 2010). Consequently, as an educator working in virtual environments, they need to understand how to build a level of trust as a function of social capital, which supports learning. To help with fuller comprehension of this problem, this dissertation provides a review of existing research, and a synopsis of the pertinent research issues.

The Philosophical Framework. In qualitative studies, the worldview assumptions the researcher brings to the study inform the design. Though philosophical ideas usually remain hidden in research (Slife & Williams, 1995), the philosophical framework will still influence the practice of research, and thus needs to be identified (Creswell, 2009). The conceptual framework for this study was derived from the expanded Mathieu et al. (2006) inputs–processes–outcomes (the investigator-P-O) model. This framework is appropriate for a qualitative analysis, as it will advise how data was collected and analyzed. Additionally, Mathieu et al.'s method was an appropriate method to use in looking for pattern identification in a nascent area (Edmondson & McManus, 2007).

For this reason, the goal was first to identify the behaviors and factors involved in creating trust in the virtual world environments used for education, and then to develop recommendations to assist learning in these environments. The intent of the research was to develop a better understanding of how educators increase trust through a virtual world experience and positively influence group or team outcomes in this virtual environment.

The current literature, which has documented the level of social capital needed to facilitate learning in a virtual environment, spans many areas and describes *social capital* and *trust* as interchangeable terms. This study also makes use of other interchangeable terms to describe a virtual world, and the following section defines these terms.

Definition and Context of the Terms

Emerging media. Emerging media is a term for the evolving and innovative use of technology and digital content to enhance work, play, and learning; to broaden access to information, and to enrich personal connection and collaboration by eliminating the physical constraints of location and time (Ball State University, 2011).

Virtual reality (VR). Bryson (as cited in Eschenbrenner, Nah, & Siau, 2008) defines *virtual reality* as "the use of computers and human–computer interfaces to create the effect of a three dimensional world containing interactive objects with a strong sense of three-dimensional presence" (p. 92).

Virtual worlds (VW). Virtual-world environments are organized within the domain of massively multiplayer online games (MMOGs). Unstructured 3-D virtual worlds such as Second Life are subtypes of MMOGs, and have been tagged with the label *multiuser virtual environments* (MUVEs; Mennecke et al., 2008, Tuten, 2009). Many scholars have used the term *virtual world* in their literature (Bell, 2008), yet there is still not a commonly applied definition. Academics, industry professionals, and the media use this term in different ways at different times.

Virtual worlds can be described as computer-simulated environments with their own physical and biological laws, populated by dynamic interacting entities such as artificial creatures and human avatars. Whereas virtual reality largely focuses on the design of 3-D immersive spaces, and artificial life on the modeling and study of lifelike systems, virtual worlds embrace both dimensions by synthesizing an entire digital universe (Heudin, 2000).

For the purposes of this study, the investigator defined a virtual world as a 3-D synchronous simulated environment facilitated by a computer network that consists of a persistent network of people, who perceive themselves as interactive parts of the environment and are represented by avatars.

Second Life (SL). This research utilized the virtual world environment, or rather the 3-D Internet environment known as Second Life (SL). Developed by Linden Lab, this program enables its users, called "Residents," to interact with each other through avatars, providing an advanced level of a social network service combined with general aspects of a metaverse. Residents are represented in the virtual world by 3-D animated agents, which are able to take whatever form and appearance a user desires. Residents can operate in many of the ways we do in real life, including interacting with other avatars, which can walk, fly, teleport, build objects, and own property and objects (Davidson, 2008).

Virtual world as a learning environment. Several educators have turned to Virtual worlds to explore the potential this medium offers for peer-to-peer learning, formal instruction, informal knowledge sharing, and co-created learning (Cooper, 2009; Ondrejka, 2008). Many software platforms have combined with SL to offer implementations for these technologies in an education context.

Furthermore, Jelen and Orel (2010) conducted a study in which they evaluated how SL is used as a learning environment in higher education, and they were able to support the assertion that the benefits of education in virtual worlds include a sense of presence, immediacy, movement, artifacts, and communication unavailable within traditional Internet-based learning environments. Additionally, the researchers noted that instructors and trainers are able to interact with their students in more fluid and natural ways (Eschenbrenner et al., 2008; Jelen & Orel, 2010).

The typical distance education experience, although often quite valuable, still lags far behind the face-to-face classroom experience (Nesson & Nesson, as cited in Jelen & Orel, 2010). Furthermore, some problems with typical distance education platforms are that visitors are usually unaware of the presence of other simultaneous visitors, and that these platforms make it unlikely that one visitor-student will contact another, even with courseware that allows students to see whether others are logged in (Nesson & Nesson, as cited in Jelen & Orel, 2010). Additionally, as Brown and Bell (as cited in Nesson & Nesson, 2008) documented, the ability of students to see each other, as well as objects and resources within the environment, provides a context for discussion, making discussion flow more easily. As Dickey (2005) cited, benefits of learning in such an environment include being able to experiment without concern for real-world repercussions and being able to learn by doing; Ondrejka (as cited in Eschenbrenner et al., 2008) mentioned, as well, a greater level of comfort among students in asking questions and an ability to develop a sense of shared learning within a group. Conway (as cited in Eschenbrenner et al., 2008) cited that the virtual environment could provide opportunities to introduce more creativity into the classroom.

Virtual teams. Powell, et al. (2004) use the term "team" in its stricter sense, adopting a widely accepted definition (p.7):

> A team is a collection of individuals who are interdependent in their tasks, who share responsibility for outcomes, who see themselves and who are seen by others as an intact social entity embedded in one or more larger social systems, and who manage their relationship across organizational boundaries. (Cohen & Baily, 1997, p. 241, as cited in Powell).

This definition is general enough to capture traditional as well as virtual teams, while precisely identifying the defining features of a team: its unity of purpose, its identity as a social structure, and its members' shared responsibility for outcomes. Therefore, virtual teams can be defined as groups of geographical and/or time dispersed students brought together by technologies to accomplish one or more common tasks (Alavi & Yoo, 1997; DeSanctis & Poole, 1997; Jarvenpaa & Leidner, 1999). Distinctive features of virtual teams include their preponderant — and at times exclusive — reliance on IT for members' communication, their flexible composition, and their ability, if necessary, to traverse traditional boundaries and time constraints (Powell, et al. 2004). Virtual teams are often assembled in response to specific needs, and are often short-lived (Chase, 1999). This is not a defining characteristic of the virtual team, but rather a byproduct of the specialized function they often serve.

Social capital. Putnam (1995) defined *social capital* as "features of social organizations such as networks, norms, and social trust that facilitate coordination and cooperation for mutual benefit" (p. 67).

Trust. Kini and Choobineh (1998) defined *trust* as "a belief in the system characteristics, specifically belief in the competence, dependability and security of the system, under conditions of risk" (p. 51). Therefore, to facilitate learning in a virtual environment, participants need to trust the system, or in this case, the technology and the organization supporting the technology. Within the multidimensional construct of trust, it is beneficial to define the key defining characteristics of trust: 1) a positive psychological and emotional state; 2) a certain expectation of another's motives, ability, fair behavior, or intentions of behavior; 3) a specific expectation regardless of the ability to monitor or control the other party; 4) ability to allow vulnerability under conditions of risk; 5) dependence on another that varies based on the task, situation, and the other person or people; and 6) a combination of trusting intentions and trusting beliefs (Boon & Holmes, 1991; Barney & Hansen, 1994; Holton, 2001; Blomqvist, 2002, Yu, et al., 2012). Based on these key factors from published research, this dissertation broadly defined ***trust*** as *a mental state in which a subject, exposed to conditions of risk, maintains an expectation of another's motives, abilities, and reasonable behavior, and displays a willingness to depend on another, regardless of the subject's ability to monitor or control the other party.* The investigator in this study expanded upon this definition somewhat to treat trust more as an observable phenomenon occurring when a person who is in a position to facilitate learning embodies personal values such as integrity, humility, compassion, and altruism, thereby modelling an example of someone who can be trusted, relied upon, and admired. Trust was demonstrated through behavior, whether in the individual's ethics, compassionate words or actions, or respectful treatment of others (Grant, 2008; Reave, 2005). Thus, the main focus of trust in this study was on the interpersonal behaviors and dynamics between educator and student.

Collaborative learning. Konstantinidis, Tsiatsos, and Pomportsis (2009) provided a descriptive definition of the collaborative virtual learning environment:

> Collaborative Learning is a general term used for the description of educational practices based on the simultaneous cognitive and mental effort of multiple students or/and educators. Students share a common goal, depend on each other and are mutually responsible for their success or failure. (p. 280)

This description of the CL environment and the role educators have in this environment was critical to this study, because the investigator was asserting that the creation of trust facilitates a collaborative learning environment. In other words, the investigator theorized that trust was a key variable in the group outcome of collaborative and other learning in virtual environments.

Significance of the Study

This research presents important findings for several areas, including education, research, and business. The significance of this study aligns with Martins et al.'s (2004) contention that trust was a determining factor in the effectiveness of groups to reach agreed-on outcomes. Put simply, for a group to achieve its goal, interpersonal trust must be present. As the use of virtual worlds increase, further understanding will be required of how best to use these environments to achieve objectives. Additionally, virtual worlds and education is an area of research still in its early stage, and it thus lacks a strong body of traditional substantiating findings (Schultze & Orlikowski, 2010). The investigator asserts that understanding the emergent aspects of these virtual worlds and their implications for organizations requires both new theories and new methods (Boje et al., 2004). Additionally, there is a call for research that explores the value and fit of virtual worlds for business and organizational needs as well as educational applications (Bendoly, Thomas, & Capra, 2010; Kim & Lee, 2010; Kennedy, Vozdolska, & McComb, 2010). These virtual environments have revealed emerging possibilities, yet they remain largely unexplored (Davis, et al., 2009; Williams, 2010). Wasko et al. (2011) found that it was important to answer questions regarding learning and collaboration in virtual worlds. Furthermore, their study supported the idea that there was a lack of prior research in the 3-D context. They also asserted that research focusing on aspects of 3-D immersion — how it is achieved, and outcomes in behaviors, attitudes, and/or intentions that result from being immersed or fully engaged in virtual world activities — is worthy of exploration. Greater understanding of how virtual worlds affect groups is warranted (Kaplan & Haenlein, 2009; Kennedy et al., 2010). Lastly, virtual worlds can support learning processes (Calongne, 2008). In fact, there has been evidence that virtual worlds are not only an emerging method of enhancing learning outcomes, but may also be even more effective than face-to-face modalities (Wiecha, Heyden, Sternthal, & Merialdi, 2010).

The investigator incorporated educator stories into this study, as the educators' describe the experiences that prompted them to integrate trust building into their virtual classrooms. There was wisdom to gain from these stories and experiences, which researchers can use to enhance the practice of facilitating collaborative learning environments. This signals significance not only for higher-education institutions, but also for organizations seeking to employ trust as a mechanism for virtual teams in training, and the collecting of these stories offered ample opportunity to investigate team processes in a virtual world setting used for learning and collaboration (Wasko, Teigland, Leidner, & Jarvenpaa, 2011). Over the past few years, the investigator has explored the literature on the subject of trust in virtual teams; using storytelling, the investigator then interwove educators' experiences with the current literature to form this study.

Assumptions and Dependencies

The study relies heavily on the current literature in several fields. Because of the disparate research in numerous interdisciplinary areas, it was necessary to make certain assumptions that the findings are generalizable across several fields. Interpersonal trust is a complex topic, and there are often inconsistencies in the literature with regard to trust concepts. Trust is a multi-dimensional construct, and there are variations in definitions of trust and its components (Hakonen & Lippon, 2009; Zolin et al., 2004; D. Owens, 2012). This study addressed these inconsistencies by clarifying the definitions. It has been assumed that the mature bodies of research from virtual teams and trust studies applied to the current study. Additionally, this study was dependent upon volunteer sample groups, which could result in biased findings. Furthermore, bias may be present in the participants' descriptions of their experiences with teaching in virtual worlds, and in their perceptions of the trust that facilitates a positive learning environment. The risks, or in other words, the study's success was contingent upon (a) the participant honestly responding to the questions in the interview; (b) the participant having successfully created trust; (c) the participant having had a positive teaching experience with SL; (d) the participant, regardless of background, providing a balanced study; and (e) the investigator following sound study methods.

Limitations and Constraints

The primary limitation was that this study is open to interpretations contrary to those intended by the investigator. The research may be too specific, and would therefore not be generalizable, owing largely to the limits of the participant sample size. The target population was limited to those educators who believed in the potential value of virtual learning environments and who had experience with building trust in these environments. The study environment was another limitation, since it was focused on the VW of Second Life, which is just one of many technologies being used for higher education purposes. While many other types of multiuser technologies could have been examined, doing so within this study would have been impractical due to resource constraints. Also, while the topic of virtual worlds in higher education has broadened to include other virtual environment platforms in which other institutions have had a measure of success, Second Life currently represents the largest group of universities and educators. Organizations such as the New Media Consortium provided a real life application and educational developments in Second Life, and expect continued growth of educational gaming and simulation (NMC, 2012). The limited scope of this study was deliberate, as this research sought to uncover the underlying themes of the role of trust in virtual learning.

There could be a perspective of bias in the study because of the construction of the method. The following methods proposed by Creswell (2003) were thus used to minimize bias: (a) triangulation of different data sources through surveys, interviews, and literature review; (b) peer debriefing to improve accuracy and to hold the investigator accountable by asking questions to clarify results; (c) editing to review the project and assess the format of the paper; and (d) reliance on the advice and experience of the chair of the dissertation committee and solicitation of committee-member feedback.

As the research design was the most likely potential threat to the study conclusions, the investigator utilized Boje's (2001a, 2001b, 2007) deconstruction and restoring methods to identify the subordinate and hierarchical voices in the stories. By using microstoria techniques (Boje, 2002, 2008, 2011a), the investigator was able to identify and analyze the predetermined ideas she brought to the research.

To validate the accuracy of information data analysis, field notes were transcribed by the investigator and then read (this included categorization, summarization, and checking; notes accompanied any multimedia to guarantee that nothing had been overlooked; Creswell, 2009). Then the data was codified via a detailed analysis and coding process, which included analyzing transcribed notes, gaining a broad sense of the interpretation of the literature, organizing the notes into theme clusters, and labeling the themes (color, topic, words; Creswell, 2009).

Summary

This chapter briefly covered the history and background of the use of emerging media such as virtual environments in an educational context. This background accounts for the development of emerging sociotechnical advancements that have given rise to educational practices using virtual environments. Trust had been shown to be particularly important to learning, and to the interpersonal relationships formed in virtual environments. The purpose of this qualitative study is to describe how educators using emerging media recognized trust as a component of social capital in virtual environments. The goal is to identify the behaviors that created trust and to develop recommendations to assist learning and explore what educators can do to help students learn in a virtual classroom. This study seeks to address deficiencies evident in the published research thus far, and to contribute a qualitative analysis to address the deficiencies by helping to further understanding of the perception of the role of trust in virtual classrooms. This analysis has built a rich, detailed description of the role of trust in the virtual world environment for educators. The study has identified similarities and differences among studies focusing on virtual worlds. The present research explored the concept of a *learning environment* and how social capital can cause the educator to succeed or fail in facilitating the learning experience in virtual worlds. To this end, the investigator sought to combine themes from educator stories that described these factors.

Chapter 2 introduces research from the literature, and summarizes past research and the gaps in current research in several disciplines. It also provides a meta-synthesis across diverse interdisciplinary areas, which explains trust, virtual worlds, virtual teams, and collaborative learning environments, and the need for further research in this area. This literature review helps to present the need for and value of this study.

Chapter II: Literature Review

The 21st century has seen human society grow more connected than ever before with the use of new technologies. This phenomenon of the growth of the networked world and subsequent changes in the way we communicate were the starting points for this research. The topic is broad, spanning many disciplines. It is apparent that the use of emerging technologies is continually increasing and changing, and this has implications for cultural, economic, political, and personal communications (Boellstroff, 2010; Hicks et al., 2009). This literature review sought to analyze emerging technologies, and the subset of emerging media, critically in their uses across disciplines to develop the broadest possible body of scholarship exploring the use of virtual environments for education. In this context, it will be possible to explore novel issues in a qualitative way, and also link them to the classic dilemmas of social analysis (Boellstroff, 2008).

Context

This study began with the premise that educators must adapt the ways in which they communicate in order to remain relevant and make the differences they want to make in others' lives. Negroponte coined the statement that "computing is not about computers any more. It is about living" (p. 6). Computers have produced an emerging media setting that creates incredible opportunities. This research thus sought to explore the ways in which higher education is using these technologies. Education, specifically the learning environment, is enhanced by elements such as social capital, trust, and collaboration. As well, virtual learning environments, such as classrooms set in the virtual world of SL, are an emerging medium that will allow formal education to remain relevant while also adapting to the issues of accessibility with growing globalization.

Many issues and complications still exist with the use of emerging media, however. The primary complication in examining emerging media is that they span several areas, including media studies and communication, sociology, cultural studies, education, and management. With such diverse viewpoints and ranges of tactics in play, current studies should examine further the evolving and emerging strategies for these media, which have been shaped by the logic and pressures of American consumption culture (Wenner, 2010). Therefore, this dissertation takes an interdisciplinary global view of the use of emerging media to examine existing literature, identifies the research gaps that exist, and subsequently completes a study that contributes to the current body of knowledge.

Emerging Media

Emerging media are forcing us to reconsider how we think about communications. New approaches are needed to identify how technological change is perceived in the context of the diverse nature of modern societies, which do not correspond neatly to national boundaries. According to Priest (2008), reactions to emerging media are better understood as a function of what audiences bring to the interpretation of news and information than as a function of exposure to message content itself. According to Priest (2008),

> beliefs and values also influence responses to media messages in crucially significant ways. Diverse "publics" in both Canada and the US — as well as elsewhere around the globe — bring distinct values, expectations and assumptions, both to their engagement with science and technology and to their interpretation of media messages. (p. 877)

Emerging media have begun to show up in many higher education institutions, including Colorado Technical University (CTU). However, CTU is not the only such institution focusing on this emerging area of research. Ball State's Emerging Media Initiative has also been successful in securing several innovation grants in this discipline (Ball State University, 2011). Leaders in this field, such as Jenkins (2006, 2011), are also researching the relevancy of *new media* in two senses: one is focused specifically on digital and mobile technologies, the wave of emerging communication tools and practices that have emerged over the past few decades, whereas the other is focused on the process by which any emerging media technology is absorbed into the culture.

Additionally, several hybrid practices have emerged that use several forms of media at the same time. Harty and Whyte (2010) studied this phenomenon using insights from actor network theory to articulate the delegation of actions to material and digital objects within ecologies of practice. The three vignettes that they identified discuss this delegation of actions as the "plugging" and "patching" of ecologies occurring across media and the continual iterations of working practices among different types of media. By shifting the focus from media silos to these wider ecologies of practice. The actor network theory approach has significant managerial implications for the stabilization of new technologies and practices and for managing technological change.

History of virtual worlds, MMOGs, and MUVEs. Organizational efforts to use virtual worlds were initially focused only on external marketing and product activities (Lu, Chiang, Lin, & Lee, 1998). These environments have been designed for a variety of functions as well as a diverse set of target markets. Virtual world research has its origins in computing science, engineering, and other applied technological sciences, with a focus on the creation and enhancement of virtual 3-D environments (Messinger et al., 2009). Davidson (2008) stated that

> SL may be one of the most widely publicized, vigorously debated, and misunderstood technologies to emerge on the information technology scene in many years. Often referred to as a game, which it is not, SL is a virtual community in which real-life people from around the world participate continuously in a great social, economic, and cultural experiment. (p. 1)

Second Life is an Internet-based virtual world that gained international attention in the media in 2006 for its virtual economy and educational uses (Castronova, 2001). Residents of virtual worlds are interested in having fun; they can explore, socialize, participate in individual and group activities, and create and trade items (conduct business) and services with one another (Davidson, 2008; Robbins & Bell, 2008).

Some virtual world environments, such as SL, Kaneva, and CityScape, are general-purpose and targeted at adults and educational environments, while others, such as SCF's virtual world, are specifically tailored to autistic children. Twinity, Kaneva, and Sulake Labs's Habbo Hotel focus on specific ages, demographics, and functional applications (Uribe, Larach, & Cabra, 2010).

Virtual world environments are organized within the domain of MMOGs. Unstructured 3-D virtual worlds, such as SL, Kaneva, There.com, and Active Worlds, as subtypes of MMOGs, have been tagged with the label MUVE (Mennecke et al., 2008; Tuten, 2009). Their design and realization require competency in various fields, from virtual reality and physics to artificial life and ecology, computer graphics, high-performance computing, and others. Owing to their nature, virtual worlds have many applications in 3-D simulation, computer games, and online business. However, the Virtual World approach is broader still, and more fundamental. Working in the context of a virtual world also addresses the problem of clarifying the constitutive principles by which large numbers of interacting elements can self-organize and produce emergent phenomena as they are observed in the natural world. Therefore, the study of virtual worlds in the past, has been mainly concerned with the formal basis of synthetic universes, and offered a promising new way to contribute to the understanding of nature and complex systems in general (Heudin, 2000).

In Second Life, a scripting language, called LSL attaches behaviors to objects, which can have associated digital rights that make it possible for one resident to create an object and allow another to copy it, thereby allowing residents to form relationships with one another and engage in virtually any type of transaction or interaction imaginable. Residents communicate with one another by typing local public chat messages or private, global instant messages, and even with voice. Although principally a visual experience and somewhat cartoonish, the experience can be quite vivid and realistic, and the extent to which participants cross the digital divide can sometimes make it difficult to distinguish between what is virtual and what is real (Davidson, 2008; Thompson, 2011).

These environments have grown dramatically in popularity (Davis et al., 2009). This growth is due in part to the immersive, 3-D environments that give users engaging opportunities and provide ready-made social communities (Kaplan & Haenlein, 2009). Consequently, many institutions have turned to virtual worlds to provide an immersive experience for students. According to Franceschi et al. (2009), because these worlds offer students the chance to share the quasi-realism of a 3-D environment in which participants can see and hear one another, as well as the capability to manipulate artifacts together, this environment presents an opportunity for a collaborative learning environment (p. 73).

Additionally, this method of instruction has very promising prospects, as Wiecha et al. (2010) showed in their study, which reported that the virtual-world method of continuing medical education was superior to the face-to-face method. Additionally, their research supported that

> the enriched environment, convenience, and possibilities for constructivist approaches all add up to tremendous potential. What's more, it is expected that virtual worlds will become more ubiquitous in other types of computing. Some speculate that virtual worlds will soon replace our Internet browsers. (p. 1)

These factors provide a strong sense of group presence, which leads to engaging group learning interactions (Franceschi et al., 2009). Furthermore, Tuten (2009) has shown that by applying the principles of authentic assessment, students are able to translate their virtual world experiences into real-world practice.

Virtual worlds in emerging media. According to Chambers (as cited in Friedman, 1999), "the next big killer application for the Internet is going to be education. Education over the Internet is going to be so big it is going to make email usage look like a rounding error" (p. A29). Additionally, Petrakou (2010) asserted that online education is gradually becoming a viable alternative to traditional campus education owing to the rapid development of information technology. Because little empirical research on virtual teams in virtual-world education has been done, generalizable, organizational studies informed this research. Schultze and Orlikowski (2010) asserted that "understanding the emergent aspects of these virtual worlds and their implications for organizations [has] required both new theories and new methods" (p. 821). Additionally, there is a call for research that explores the value and fit of virtual worlds for business and organizational needs as well as educational applications (Bendoly et al., 2010; Kim & Lee, 2010; Kennedy et al., 2010).

In the emerging e-commerce domain, Rindova, Petkova, and Kotha (2007) conducted a study examining a model that relates the visible external actions of three firms to the patterns of media coverage they accumulated.

Rindova et al. found that, given the limited theory and empirical evidence about the process of reputation accumulation by new firms in emerging markets, patterns of media coverage are likely both to reflect and affect the process of reputation accumulation:

> The media constitute an influential audience of critics, who first form their own perceptions and opinions, thereby reflecting the process of reputation accumulation, and then disseminate these perceptions and opinions to the public, thereby influencing the perceptions and opinions of other stakeholder audiences (p. 43).

Rindova et al.'s analysis indicated that the pattern of market actions of new firms does in fact influence the pattern of media coverage received in terms of level (visibility), content (strategic character), tenor (favorability), and distinction (esteem). Finally, the study suggested that reputation might be better understood as a composite construct and those reputational assets may vary in their composition (Rindova et al., 2007).

Virtual environments are yet another form of new media that has potential and use. Yet, they remain a largely unexplored field, in both business and educational contexts (Davis et al., 2009; Williams, 2010). Additionally, a greater understanding of how virtual worlds affect groups is warranted (Kaplan & Haenlein, 2009; Kennedy et al., 2010). Focusing primarily on these opportunities for further research, this study seeks to tie educational groups operating in virtual worlds to team performance.

Virtual teams. Traditionally, both the terms "team" and "group" have been used to describe small collections of people working together. While these words are often used interchangeably in traditional and virtual team research (Cohen & Baily, 1997; Langfred, 1998; Sundstrom et al., 1990), this duality in terminology has increasingly been questioned (Fisher et al., 1997; Katzenbach & Smith, 1993). Several authors suggest that the term "team" should be reserved for those groups that display high levels of interdependency and integration among members. This study recognizes this distinction and uses the term "team" in its stricter sense, adopting a widely accepted definition: "A team is a collection of individuals who are interdependent in their tasks, who share responsibility for outcomes, who see themselves and who are seen by others as an intact social entity embedded in one or more larger social systems, and who manage their relationship across organizational boundaries" (Cohen & Baily, 1997, p. 241). This definition is general enough to cover traditional as well as virtual teams, while precisely identifying the defining features of a team: its unity of purpose, its identity as a social structure, and its members' shared responsibility for outcomes. Powell, Piccoli, and Ives (2004) defined *virtual teams* "as groups of geographically, organizationally and/or time dispersed workers brought together by information and telecommunication technologies to accomplish one or more organizational tasks" (p. 7). The adoption of this definition limited the scope of the work done in this study. This study thus did not review research that focused on computer-supported collaborative workgroups that meet for one or two sessions of very limited duration, or groups in which there are no shared responsibilities for outcomes. This study defined virtual teams as groups of geographically, organizationally, and/or time-dispersed workers brought together by information and telecommunication technologies to accomplish one or more tasks (Alavi & Yoo, 1997; DeSanctis & Poole, 1997; Jarvenpaa & Leidner, 1999). While they can be ongoing, virtual teams are often assembled on an "as-needed" basis to cooperate on specific deliverables, or to fulfill specific customer needs (Chase, 1999; Lipnack & Stamps, 1997). Distinctive features of virtual teams include their preponderant — and at times exclusive — reliance on IT for internal communication, their flexible composition, and their ability, if necessary, to traverse traditional organizational boundaries and time constraints. Virtual teams are often assembled in response to specific needs and are often short-lived (Chase, 1999). This short lifespan is not a defining characteristic of the virtual team, but rather a byproduct of the specialized functions they often serve.

Learning in virtual worlds. Virtual worlds have been shown to support the learning process; *flow* is one of the attributes which contributes to this process. Csikszentmihalyi coined the term *flow* to describe the intrinsically motivated mental and emotional state characterized by intense concentration and enjoyment. It is described as the holistic, positive sensation people feel when they act with total involvement, concentration, and immersion (Csikszentmihalyi, 1990; see also 1990). Hoffman and Novak (1996) supported the hypothesis that consumers who experience flow while using the Web are more likely to retain more of what they perceive, with implications for the effectiveness of marketing communications (Bolton & Saxena-Lyer, 2009; Hoffman & Novak, 2009). Additionally, Skadberg and Kimmel (2004) found that flow was the most important factor contributing to increased learning, and that this learning, along with Web site attractiveness, was the most important factor affecting changes in attitude and behavior. Furthermore, Choi, Kim, and Kim (2007) found that the experience of flow was positively related to learning outcomes among participants in a Web-based training program. These ideas supported the use of virtual worlds in the learning process because these environments offered a unique immersive experience that had a profound influence on cognition. In addition, swift change in both organizational environments and instructional methods has forced institutions to adapt rapidly to the continuous demand for improved and updated skills that match technological advances in both content and processes of work (Akdere & Conceicão, 2006). Understanding how virtual worlds function as sites of adult learning, and what the enablers and barriers are to successful learning in a virtual world, is therefore important in understanding the complexities and potentialities of virtual worlds in a learning context (Mancuso, Chluo, & McWhorter, 2010). Many studies have indicated a positive relationship between flow and learning, achievement, and engagement (Chen, 2006; Cooper, 2009; Konradt, Filip, & Hoffmann, 2003; Shernoff, Csikszentmihalyi, Schenider, & Shernoff, 2003). Likewise, Cooper's (2009) studies indicated that flow as an engagement framework within SL supports learning. Virtual worlds offer a unique environment in which to study the underlying dimensions of flow theory in learning — for example, the use of avatars in increasing the sense of identification; manipulation of the environment in increasing the sense of control; and visualization capabilities in increasing the sense of immersion (Cooper, 2009). Despite the findings in all of these studies, however, there is very little research on the relationship between 3-D virtual environments and learning potential that stems from the immersive engagement resulting from flow. As well, using virtual worlds in this manner does raise some additional questions. Many researchers agree that future studies should included how well students function in virtual constructs; How virtual-world technology supports learning; and how trust affect outcomes in virtual environments (Kirkman & Mathieu, 2005; Marks, Mathieu, & Zaccaro, 2001; Martins et al., 2004; Messinger et al., 2009). The virtual-world environment as a learning context is thus an important setting for further research.

Many researchers agree that virtual teams can be used in virtual worlds for learning purposes, and they have shown the importance of collaborative work (Kimball, 1997; Metcalf & Dede, 2011; Noble, 2002). Co-creation and collaboration are key factors in the virtual learning process. There exist several opportunities to explore in what way and how virtual worlds facilitate learning (Riggs & Shimmin, 2008). Insight drawn from specific studies of virtual worlds used in the workplace, such as in contexts of training and collaboration, needs to be explored (Benford, Greenhalg, Rodden, & Pycock, 2001). The relationships among these dimensions, especially in virtual worlds, is important in creating an engaging learning experience, and is thus an important aspect for future investigation. The matter of how virtual worlds can sharpen more orthodox forms of communication has not been fully investigated either (Bellman & Landauer, 2000; Ubell, 2010). Last, there also exists a need for research on how virtual worlds relate to emergent trends such as social networking, online economies, virtual businesses, and online culture, and their impact on business (Messinger et al., 2009).

Emerging media such as immersive virtual environments are influential and blooming sites for education purposes (Bell, 2008; Boland, 2009; Robbins, 2007), and the subject of much interest (Air Educational and Training Command, 2008; Cooper, 2009; Allen, 2007; Wyld, 2008). The attention of educators looking to further their understanding of this technology is also compelling (KZERO, 2008; Levy, 2008). Many studies have supported the findings that virtual worlds support learning and that flow and collaboration are attributes that contribute to the learning process (Chen, 2006; Cooper, 2009; Konradt et al., 2003; Metcalf & Dede, 2011; Noble, 2002; Shernoff et al., 2003). Overall, virtual teams functioning in virtual-world educational environments are critical to successful group outcomes in virtual-world educational environments and warrant further examination (Calongne, 2008; Cooper, 2009). This study asserts that a key part of ensuring team success in these contexts is the building of social capital and, specifically, trust.

Trust

Researchers increasingly recognize that observers' perceptions of and beliefs about an organization have a substantive effect on the organization's access to resources and performance. However, the processes through which these perceptions form are not well understood (Rindova et al., 2007). In terms of education, according to Coppola, Hiltz, and Rotter (2004), "establishing swift trust at the beginning of an online course appears to be related to subsequent course success" (p. 95). Meyerson, Weick, and Kramer (1996) developed the concept of *swift trust* for temporary teams that form around a clear purpose and common task and have a finite life span. Many scholars have studied the dimensions and outcomes of trust as a component of social capital. When comparing trust in virtual environments to trust in physical settings, it has been found that over time, trust in virtual settings will rise to levels that meet or exceed the levels of trust in face-to-face teams (Wilson, et al., 2006; Owen, 2012). This is particularly important as lower levels of trust will affect team performance (Jarvenpaa, et al., 2004). While trust levels tend to rise over time, high levels of early trust can protect virtual team members from some of the unpredictable and chaotic processes that are characteristic of virtual team interaction (Jarvenpaa et al., 2004, Owens, 2012). A general disposition to trust, a greater familiarity with the community, and a stronger norm of reciprocity in communication within the community may increase the level of trust placed in a virtual community; this assertion warrants further research (Casalo, Flavian, & Guinaliu, 2008; Mancuso et al., 2010). The dynamic of social capital and trust in virtual environments used specifically for education is relatively unexplored, and thus also merits more investigation (Davis et al., 2009; Schultze & Orlikowski, 2010; Williams, 2010).

Social capital. Claridge (2004) asserts that, for substantive and ideological reasons, social capital does not have a clear, undisputed meaning (Dolfsma & Dannreuther, 2003; Foley & Edwards, 1997). Additionally, researchers have studied the concept of social capital and its role in the ways communities and families interact (Coleman, 1988 & Putnam, 2000). While social capital has been thought of as a positive influence, providing individuals with the social resources that can enhance their life experience, researchers remain at odds with each other on many aspects of social capital. Woolcock (1998) stated that social capital is a broad term encompassing the "norms and networks facilitating collective actions for mutual benefits" (p. 155). Given this expansive definition, social capital is often misunderstood and misrepresented. For this reason, there is no commonly agreed-upon definition of social capital, and the particular definition adopted by a study will depend on the discipline and level of investigation (Robison, Schmid, & Siles, 2002). This study used Putnam's (1995) definition of social capital, offered in chapter one, as meaning "features of social organization such as networks, norms, and social trust that facilitate coordination and cooperation for mutual benefit" (p. 67). Social capital has also been applied to the Internet as a concept of "maintained social capital," referring to "online network tools which enable individuals to keep in touch with a social network after physically disconnecting from it" (Ellison et al., 2007, p. 1). As stated before, the concept of trust is complex and multifaceted. Not only do people need to trust the emerging technology (as secure and reliable), but they also need to have a level of trust with each other to facilitate learning (Kilpatrick, Field, & Falk, 2003). Trust has been shown to be a key component of social capital, and there is a mature body of research on which to draw in this regard. In the existing research, trust as a component of social capital serves as a "social relation that has productive benefits" (Adler & Kwon, 2002; Field, 2005; Robison et al., 2002). Therefore, to illustrate the role of trust in social capital, a multi-level analytical lens of trust factors (Mayer, et al., 1995) and shared repertoire (Wenger, 1998) has been integrated into the ontology underlying this study, as it reflects the viewpoint that human perceptions shape actions and social reality, and that complex social phenomena in virtual worlds are best understood through interaction between researcher and virtual educators. The role of social capital can be visualized as both a cause and effect in a circular flow, as depicted below (adapted from Resnick, 2001).

Trust in virtual worlds. Among the most important developments facing theorists and managers are emerging technologies such as virtual worlds, and the methods by which to facilitate trust and virtual collaboration within them (Dourish, 2001, Duarte & Tennant - Snyder, 1999; Kahn, 2005, Francovich, et al., 2008). Empirical research has shown that trust is built behaviorally (Brothers, 1995; Reina & Reina, 2006). The behaviors that build trust are as real in a virtual world as they are in the physical face-to-face world; they create conditions that enhance collaboration in either the face-to-face or virtual modalities. A high level of trust tends to make both communication and collaboration easier, and trust is just as vital in virtual relationships as it is in local relationships (Francovich, et al., 2008).

Researchers suggest that social interaction is created around a commitment among virtual community members to exchange knowledge and experiences. While the exchange of knowledge and experiences among different members does not necessarily produce trust, it does expose people to the possibility of connecting with each other and to the development of social ties, and trust is negotiated because of these ties (Daniel et al., 2002; Wenger, 2001). In an educational context, educators using Second Life also commonly cite presence, interactivity and engagement as their key motivations, which are all also connected to trust (Bowers et al., 2009). With the increase in the use of virtual worlds for education, the study of the processes and functions of the motivations for using virtual worlds been identified as a nascent area of research (Davis, 2010). Recent research has explored the correlation among a number of identified parameters, including presence, immersion, and emotion, but the study of trust in these environments is still unexplored (Banos, et al., 2004).

Trust in virtual teams. Trust has been studied extensively within the construct of face to face environments, and has been shown to be a determining feature in effectiveness of team outcomes(Martins et al., 2004). Trust is also a key factor in virtual teams (Handy, 1995; Jarvenpaa et al., 1998; Sarker et al., 2010), because an environment with high trust minimizes the adverse impact that geographic distribution can have on psychological intimacy (Beranek & Martz, 2005; Warkentin & Beranek, 1999; Walther, 1997). In teams with short-term lifespans, Giddens (1991) coined the term *time-space distanciation*, and asserted that an ongoing space for building trust-based relations is needed. Additionally, in another type of virtual team environment, Wenger et al. (2002) also asserted that Communities of Practice, or CoPs, are precisely such a stable element in an ever-changing organization. Though CoPs may increase trust in specific interpersonal relations by allowing ongoing communication among individuals, they may also be able to increase the level of trust through swift trust mechanisms.

Swift trust was introduced by Meyerson, Weick, & Kramer (1996) as a concept through which to explain findings indicating that teams of people who have never met may still exhibit trust behaviors. Although swift trust is fragile and temporary, studies have indicated that high levels of swift trust do provide performance advantages for virtual project teams (Robert et al., 2009; Kanawattanachai & Yoo, 2002; Javenpaa & Leidner, 1999; Zolin, Hinds, Fruchter, & Levitt, 2004). However, these studies have not examined how levels of swift trust can be raised, nor do they offer solutions to overcome the temporal and fragile nature of swift trust in short-term teams. The implications of if the team is short-lived that the trust may be too is warranted for examination. The research design proposed in the next section examines a virtual CoP as a facilitator of both swift trust and trust built through personal interaction.

Some of the determining factors in establishing trust in the virtual environment have been studied by various researchers to examine how time, communication intensity, and the ability to cope with technical and task uncertainty (Ratcheva & Vyakarnam, 2001; Walther, 1995; Walther & Burgoon, 1992) relate to affective outcomes (Martins et al., 2004). In support of these findings, several attributes of communication have been found to facilitate the formation of trust within virtual teams (Jarvenpaa & Leidner, 1999). The past research in this area can be grouped into three main categories: (a) the role of trust in face-to-face teams; (b) the positive effects of trust on long-term group performance; and (c) the constructs of the virtual teams (short-term/long-term). Virtual team research is new. Most of the prior research in this area has focused on applying the findings from research into traditional teams to the virtual environment (Kirkman & Mathieu, 2005; Marks et al., 2001; Martins et al., 2004). The majority of the literature has focused on the short-term effects of trust, and current theories are limited to small sample environments (Cohen & Gibson, 2003; De Jong & Elfring, 2010). As well, a large part of the research has focused on correlation, and does not study all the variables in relation to each other (Gibson & Manuel, 2003; Jarvenpaa, Knoll, & Leidner, 1998; Martins et al., 2004).

Related Practitioner Research

In the area of practice, there are several instances of literature on "strategies for building trust in virtual environments," as this topic has gained more attention with the organizational move to using virtual teams in operations. However, there is little empirical evidence to support these strategies. Many practitioners and scholars alike recognize that trust is a key component of team success, whether virtual or face-to-face. The investigator asserts that virtual team management, and building trust within a team (including a group of students or a group of employees), is critical to reaching positive outcomes. According to Serrat (2009),

> when they are effective, teams are typified by intelligibility of purpose, trust, open communication, clear roles, the right mix of talent and skills, full participation, individual performance, quality control, risk taking, collective delivery of products and services, an appropriate level of sponsorship and resources, and balanced work-life interactions. (p. 55)

While the stages of team development are the same regardless of environment, the similarities between face-to-face teams and virtual teams end there. Teams that operate in the virtual environment raise unique challenges for educators and managers alike, challenges that academic literature and organizational practice are only just beginning to explore. Serrat explored some strategies for building trust in virtual environments:

> To appear and develop, it requires that certain conditions be met, such as a shared culture, social context, and values; physical proximity; information exchange; and time. Most of these conditions are not easily met in the context of virtual teams. In a virtual environment, trust is based more on (ability and) delivery of the task at hand than on interpersonal relationships. (p. 56)

Porter (as cited in Elliot, 2007) found that building trust in a virtual community calls for more than interesting content and incentives. She asserted that consumers must be provided with quality content that is useful, relevant, and timely. To leverage consumers' fascination with online interaction, we should keep in mind the foundation of any good relationship: trust (Porter, 2007).

Related Academic Studies

From the academic perspective, the potential advantages of using virtual environments to overcome the barriers of face-to-face prejudice, develop social skills, and increase cognitive flexibility have been an area of focus. Success depends on trust building, which is difficult to achieve in a computer-mediated environment that may be conducive only to selected intercultural contexts (Walther, 1997). Krebs, Hobman, and Bordia (2006) found that virtual groups given an equivalent amount of time for message exchange as their face-to-face counterparts showed similar levels of trust. This pattern is consistent with Walther's (1996) SIP theory, which states that if computer-mediated groups are given enough time for message exchange, they will reach the same level of development as traditional groups. Therefore, if virtual groups are permitted sufficient time to communicate socio-emotional information, their members develop levels of trust similar to those of members of in-person groups. While there is a wealth of literature on how building trust in virtual teams is a challenge (Jarvenpaa & Leidner, 1999; Kirkman, Rosen, Gibson, Tesluk, & McPherson, 2002; Krebs et al., 2006), however, there is little supported evidence on how to do it successfully.

In light of the preceding findings, further research is needed to address theoretical gaps in the literature on the interpersonal processes educators can use to facilitate trust in a virtual environment.

Deficiencies and Need for a Qualitative Method

With the pervasive and ubiquitous nature of technology, virtual teams are becoming a more prevalent construct. However, many studies on this topic are relatively new and lack cohesion. One of the first issues that Martins et al. (2004) chose to identify was the question of what constitutes a virtual team. While several characteristics and traits have been discussed, the two most widely identified features are (a) geographic dispersion and (b) use of electronic communications (Cohen & Gibson, 2003; Griffith et al., 2003; Kirkman & Mathieu, 2005; Martins et al., 2004). It is important to understand the disagreement among scholars on what makes a virtual team, because this is one reason that much of the literature is disparate. Martins et al. (2004) took an integrative approach in defining virtual teams "as teams whose members use technology to varying degrees in working across locational, temporal, and relational boundaries to accomplish an interdependent task" (p. 808). Using this definition of virtual teams, the investigator was able to explore the affective content of trust.

Given this definition, Martins et al. (2004) suggested that many aspects of virtual team functioning remain unexamined. Most of this research has been done on uninhibited behaviors with face-to-face teams on the premise that the results are generalizable and therefore applicable to virtual teams. In other words, the outcomes of trusting relationships within virtual teams appear to be similar to those noted in traditional teams (Driscoll, 1978).

The literature has also examined trust extensively within the construct of traditional team literature, and has shown it to be a determining feature in team effectiveness (Martins et al., 2004). Additionally, researchers have noted that trust is a key factor in virtual teams (e.g., Handy, 1995; Jarvenpaa et al., 1998; Sarker et al., 2010) since trust will minimize any potential negative effects from the global distribution of the participants (Walther, 1997; Warkentin & Beranek, 1999). Researchers have thus described trust as the "glue of the global workspace" (O'Hara-Devereaux & Johansen, 1994, p. 243). In support of these findings, several attributes of team communication have been found to facilitate the formation of trust within virtual teams (Jarvenpaa & Leidner, 1999). Furthermore, Martins et al. (2004) state as part of their findings, "it has also been suggested that a face-to-face meeting during the initial 'courtship' period of a virtual team's life cycle helps develop trust in the team" (Coutu, 1998; Suchan & Hayzak, 2001). Interestingly, while high- and low-performing virtual teams may start with the same levels of trust, the high performers appear to be better able to develop and maintain those levels throughout their projects (Kanawattanachai & Yoo, 2002). A shared group identity has been suggested as critical to the effective functioning of teams owing to its impact on cooperation, commitment to decisions, and levels of trust (Kramer & Brewer, 1986). Identification may be of even greater significance within virtual teams particularly when the teams anticipate working together on further occasions in the future (Walther, 1997).

Therefore, in light of the preceding findings, Martins et al. (2004) asserted that further research is needed to address the major gaps that exist in the literature on the interpersonal processes, to include trust as one of these processes, as related to long-term group outcomes. Specifically, the role of trust in virtual teams remains an area in which there is room for extensive future research.

This study focused on two team-level processes, team monitoring and team effort (De Jong & Elfring, 2010). De Jong and Elfring were able to establish how these processes act as mediating mechanisms that together transmit the effects of trust on performance. However, they did their analysis in a face-to-face environment. The investigator proposes to study these constructs in a virtual world environment. Past studies on the mediated effects of trust have tended to focus on only one of these processes as a variable. De Jong and Elfring's examination of the mediating role of multiple team processes has provided a complete review, and has also allowed for integration and testing of alternative theories on how trust affects performance (Mathieu, DeShon, & Bergh, 2008). To evaluate effectively the affective outcomes of virtual teams, the link among the processes must be considered (classified as planning, action, and interpersonal processes; Marks et al., 2001) and group outcomes.

This study seeks to address these deficiencies with a qualitative analysis by helping to further understanding of the role of trust in virtual teams as told by educators. It does this by building a rich, detailed description of the role of trust in the virtual environment. It uses qualitative research to do so, an approach supported by the findings of Edmondson and McManus (2007), who promoted qualitative research as a means to clarify existing mature theory. While the themes of trust in teams and social capital have been studied over time with increasing precision by a variety of scholars, the studies in the field are nevertheless relatively new and lack cohesion. There is a need to explore team perceptions of the role of trust in the virtual environment, making it nascent theory. Since the role of trust has not been thoroughly explored within the virtual team environment, it may be considered an outlier, existing outside the "mean tendency." There is a need for observation and investigation to see if new patterns emerge and to suggest further work or a new theory. This research can be used to explore interactions from the viewpoints of the participants (attitudinal–psychological factors regarding trust in virtual interaction; Creswell, 2009), and achieves the best research fit methodologically (Edmondson & McManus, 2007).

Summary

There is a large amount of interest surrounding the virtual world environment among researchers and in the education community. It is apparent that emerging media has profoundly transformed society and business, and it continues to transform education. The purpose of this qualitative study is to describe how the emerging media of Second Life is used to facilitate trust as a component of social capital in virtual environments used for education. To accomplish this end, it is important to define what is meant by social capital and trust, and to understand how they carry over into the virtual environment in the context of education. The review of the literature started with a brief understanding of emerging media, and how virtual worlds are categorized in this area. The current use of virtual worlds and teams, and the research regarding learning within teams, were then explored. Definitions of trust and social capital were then explored to create a meta-synthesis of these factors in the context of virtual teams. Finally, the need for a qualitative methodology was explored, using current literature on qualitative design.

The literature review revealed that virtual worlds have been an active research topic for several years; however, the technology has not been robust enough to support intricate and multifaceted scenarios until recently. Virtual world platforms, such as Second Life, have seen a growth in use as they complement or even replace traditional learning settings (Cooper, 2009). Yet there still is not a mature body of literature illustrating the real benefits and limitations of using these technologies in relation to trust in virtual teams and group outcomes as opposed to face-to-face alternatives. This research addresses a gap in the literature to gain a deeper understanding of the educational potential of these environments, and explores how trust facilitates a collaborative learning environment and enhances team performance in virtual worlds.

The following chapter provides a description of the qualitative method used in this research. This method uses narrative analysis and storytelling to explain the trust-building experiences of educators who are using virtual worlds, and to explore their similarities and differences. The chapter describes the storytelling method, participant selection, the interview process, how the data was collected, and the validity of the study.

Chapter III: Methodology

Introduction to the Methodology

The theory regarding the influence of trust on long-term group outcomes in virtual teams is drawn from Dirks and Ferrin's (2001) moderation model of the role of trust in organizational settings, and De Jong and Elfring's (2010) findings on the mediating role of trust. The moderation model suggests that trust does not directly elicit any particular behavioral outcomes, but influences how people interpret or evaluate information related to attitudes and behavior. Dirks and Ferrin (as cited in Jarvenpaa, Shaw, & Staples, 2004) identified two explanations for the moderation effect: (a) "trust affects how one *assesses the future behavior* of another party with whom one is interdependent (or who may take action that affects oneself)" and (b) "trust also affects how one *interprets the past (or present) actions* of the other party, and the motives underlying the actions" (emphasis in text, p. 456).

Martins et al. (2004) used the Input-Process-Output or I-P-O framework from Hackman and Morris (1975) as their theoretical lens. This model has been the prevalent model applied to team studies to help interpret the factors in effective team leadership the factors in team leadership (Zaccaro & Marks, 2001) and the successful completion of team processes (Fedor et al., 2003). Specifically, the interpersonal processes, defined by Martins et al. (2004) as relationships among group members that include the tone of interaction, trust, cohesion, affect, and social integration, were the specific focus of an examination of virtual team outcomes in relation to social capital. Mathieu, Gilson, and Ruddy (2006) wanted to explore how these interpersonal processes serve to mediate the influence of empowerment on group outcomes. They felt that the I-P-O model was not expansive enough to explain team behaviors. Therefore, they modified this model, using structural equation modeling techniques. This expanded I-P-O model is used as the theoretical lens for the design of the current qualitative study. To evaluate the affective outcomes of virtual groups, the links between processes (classified as planning, action, and interpersonal processes [Marks et al., 2001]) and long-term group outcomes (Zaccaro et al., 2001) are explored. The interpersonal processes as defined by Martins et al. (2004) above are the specific focus of the examination of virtual team outcomes in relation to the role of trust and moderating effects (De Jong & Elfring, 2010). With this in mind, this research will identify the similarities and differences among various experiences of the facilitation of trust in virtual world environments used for education, in which each educator's personal experience is unique to him or her.

The research uses a qualitative methodology that involves storytelling. Denzin and Lincoln (2004) described the characteristics of a qualitative approach to research thus:

> Qualitative research is multimethod in focus, involving an interpretive, naturalistic approach to its subject matter. This means that qualitative researchers study things in their natural settings, attempting to make sense of or interpret phenomena in terms of the meanings people bring to them. (p. 5)

In an effort to "interpret the phenomena in terms of the meaning people bring to them," this study uses stories, as "stories are the blood vessels through which change pulsates in the heart of organizational life" (Boje, 1991, p. 8). Boje described storytelling as being intertextual, meaning that with each element of the tale, a line is woven in the interconnective web of stories and more stories (Boje, 2001a). Because of this, stories give a sense of the connections among networks of storytellers, with everyone crafting his or her own unique variant of experience. Yet storytelling analysis is a complex process; one story must ultimately win out over another (Boje, 2001b, 2001c, 2002), and the official story can cover over many other voices (Boje, 2010, 2011a, 2011b).

While this study uses a research method involving storytelling, this methodology can be considered a type of narrative study. Creswell (1998) offers a guide to the basic features of a phenomenological study, which, in the present case, take the following form:

1. The study reports a brief philosophical perspective of the phenomenological approach.
2. The investigator studies a single phenomenon or experience (educators' experiences with trust).
3. The investigator "brackets" preconceptions, uses open-ended questions and records experience.
4. The investigator advances specific phenomenological data analysis steps.

The word *phenomenology* describes a school of thought that focuses on a person's subjective experiences and his or her interpretations of the world. With phenomenology, the investigator sees the world through another person's eyes (Trochim, 2006). The phenomenon in such a study is structured by observation of the world around us, the experiences we have, patterns in people's behavior, and social problems we would like to alleviate (Cacioppo, et al., 2004). The focus of this study is only a fragment of the overall phenomenon, filtered through the investigator's understanding. The investigator uses phenomenological methodology to identify the human experience as described by the participants in the study. Here, the phenomenon is educators' personal experiences with trust in virtual worlds.

Since a qualitative theory cannot be developed purely from observations or incidents using raw data. The incidents, events, and happenings must be analyzed as indicators of phenomena that are given conceptual labels (Strauss & Corbin, 1990). Theory is then created when other, similar phenomena are used to form the basis of the theory, inductively derived from the study of the phenomena it represents — that is, discovered, developed, and provisionally verified through systematic data collection and analysis of data pertaining to that phenomenon (Grant, 2008).

Therefore, to identify what is relevant, generative questions, which guide the research uncover core theoretical concepts began to evolve, and a natural link between the theoretical concepts and the data develop. The final result is a core concept or category central to the research (Trochim, 2006).

Trochim's (2006) three analytic strategies were used to approach this study:

1. Coding is a process of categorizing qualitative data and describing the implications of these categories.
2. Journaling is the recording of thoughts and ideas as they evolve during the research.
3. Integrative diagrams are used to pull all of the detail together to make sense of the data with respect to the emerging theory.

Therefore, to outline further the methodology that is used to guide this research effort, this chapter (a) discusses storytelling, (b) introduces the methodology and design used here, (c) describes subject selection, (d) details the data collection process, (e) describes the interviewing process, (f) discusses the validity of the study, (g) explains the study ethics, and (h) provides a summary.

Storytelling

The problem with narrative analysis is that stories and narratives are both extremely rich and ambiguous concepts with a long and contentious pedigree in many fields related to human expression (Agar, 2005, p. 25). To analyze the art of storytelling requires a study of the collective behavior of the storytellers (Boje, 1999). According to Boje, "stories are collectively disputed, contested, and negotiated" (p. 1). Storytelling is human nature, and we mostly interact with each other through stories and not through unnarrated facts; this dyadic interaction recounts our lives in story form, not in bullet points (Grant, 2008). Riessman (1993) uses the term *first-person account of experience* when describing the storytelling encounter. Additionally, some stories are better than others; they are more coherent, truer to the way people and the world are perceived in fact and value (Fisher, 1987).

An interpretive biography can provide a narrative account for analysis (Denzin, 1989, Denzin & Lincoln, 2004). Many scholars have asserted that thoughtful analysis about stories within data enables us to think creatively about the sorts of data we collect and how we interpret them. According to Coffey and Atkinson (1996), researchers emphasize that the stories our informants tell can be seen . . . they are highly structured (and formal) ways of transmitting information (Grant, 2008). Riessman (1993) further asserted that the *interpretative turn* or the collection of stories in social science provides narrative themes as well as data for analysis.

Functions of storytelling. Denzin (1989) described a *narrative* as a story of a sequence of events that has significance for the narrator and the audience. The story has a beginning, middle, and end, as well as a logic that makes sense to the narrator (Coffey & Atkinson, 1996). However, Coffey and Atkinson (1996) contended that there is not a single form of storytelling or narrative. "Narratives and stories can be collected 'naturally'; for example, by recording stories as they occur during participant observation in a research setting" (p. 56). Riessman (1993) also noted that during research interviews, respondents often organize their responses into stories.

In storytelling, social actors talk to strangers (the investigator) to retell key experiences and events (Grant, 2008). Stories have a variety of functions. According to Coffey and Atkinson (1996), "social actors often remember and order their careers or memories as a series of narrative chronicles, that is, as series of stories marked by key happenings" (p. 56). In the life of a research project, an almost infinite number of words are spoken; a few are heard and written down, and the rest can be lost forever. Furthermore, not all the words that are heard and written down become "significant data" to be manipulated in different ways by the interpretative process (Bredo & Feinberg, 1982).

Methods of storytelling. The interpretive process of coming to understand behavior is known as "Verstehen," which is simply the very for "to understand" and describes a form of empathic and vicarious understanding, which will emerge from and through experiences and relationships with others (Jackson, cited in Lawrence-Lightfoot & Hoffman Davis, 1997). The interpretation of experience is an integral element in any qualitative research (Lancey, 1993). In narrative analysis, the object of investigation is the story itself (Riessman, 1993). The purpose is to see how respondents in interviews impose order on the flow of experience to make sense of events and actions in their lives (Riessman, 1993).

Analysis in narrative studies opens up the forms of telling about experience, not simply the content to which language refers (Grant, 2008). "We ask, why was the story told that way? Individuals become the autobiographical narratives by which they tell about their lives" (Riessman, 1993, p. 2). Telling stories about past events is a universal human activity, and one of the first forms of discourse that we learn (Nelson, 1989). Using Boje's approach, the interview process in this study poses semi-structured, open-ended questions. In asking the questions, the investigator listens with a minimum of interruption and ties the research questions back to the responses, when possible. The interview, therefore, becomes a form of conversation in that the investigator asks a question and the subject responds. It is an activity steeped in our cultural codes and in modes of intuitive and spontaneous interpretations (Grant, 2008). Through this cooperation in the research process, the investigator and subject jointly put the pieces together into a meaningful whole, something that makes sense to both, with each participant having left his or her mark on the process and the product (Richmond, 2002). This is how Kristeva (1980) puts it together:

> "The word's status is thus defined horizontally (the word in the text belongs to both writing subject and addressee) as well as vertically (the word in the text is oriented towards an anterior or synchronic literary corpus) . . . each word (text) is an intersection of words (texts) where at least one other word (text) can be read . . . any text is constructed as a mosaic of quotations; any text is the absorption and transformation of another."

Models of storytelling. Qualitative researchers seek to interpret others' experiences. According to Riessman (1993), "we cannot give voice, but we do hear voices that we record and interpret" (p. 8). Additionally, he provided a model for identifying different levels of the research process. This model includes five levels of the primary experience of an individual. When the investigator is interviewing the individual, the investigator is listening as the person begins to re-create the phenomenological experience from a stream of consciousness. During the interview process, the person travels through the following five levels as he or she re-creates the phenomenological experience: (a) attending, (b) telling, (c) transcribing, (d) analyzing, and (e) reading. Riessman (1993) goes on to describe each of the levels in this process.

First, the person attends the experience and begins to reflect, remember, and recollect his or her observations from the experience, and images come alive (Riessman, 1993). Second, the person talks about the experience through a personal narrative, which is a personal account of what happened. As the person describes his or her story, more questions are asked, and the person is encouraged to continue to describe and explain more about the experience. By listening, the researcher reaches the third level, which is transcribing records and then producing a narrative. During the process, the person telling the story will realize that there is a gap between what he or she lived through and the act of communicating the experience. As the investigator listens, a number of actions are taken to capture the person's experience. Researchers (Du Bois et al., 1993) assert that transcribing and coding are interpretive practices that can be determined by the investigator and that "theory-bound" judgments are appropriate (p.79). This leads to the fourth level, analysis. There are three main kinds of qualitative analysis strategies: categorizing (such as coding and thematic analysis), connecting (such as narrative analysis and individual case studies), and memos or displays (for more details, see Coffey & Atkinson, 1996; Dey, 1993; Maxwell, 2005). These methods can, and generally should, be combined (Maxwell, 2008, p. 236). The fifth and final process comes as the reader encounters the written report. The investigator passes around an early draft so feedback and comments can be received before the final report is produced (Grant, 2008).

Storytelling for this study. "People, it seems, are by their nature storytelling animals, and spend a fair amount of time sorting out the truth of stories" (Boje, 1999, p. 3). This study gathered stories using narrative inquiry methods. Educators' stories are collected in a one-on-one encounter through in-depth interviews. This research approach allows the educators to tell their own stories in a reasonable and recursive way.

The research provides a description of the educators' stories and experiences based on their recollections and statements about their own feelings and perspectives. The narrative process enables these educators to begin to "restory" and reconstruct their accounts in an informal setting. This approach to the research use of narratives and storytelling is self-directed. To analyze the educators' stories, the investigator uses a narrative framework that serves as a screen through which the investigator can examine the story of the educator. More important, this becomes a way for an educator to reflect critically on earlier or current perspectives to construct or reconstruct meaning in his or her life world.

As mentioned before, the word *story* is used interchangeably with *narrative* throughout this study. The stories of educators reflect "a kind of life story" that enables us to study "how humans make meaning of experience by endlessly telling and retelling stories about themselves" (Connelly & Clandinin, 1990, p. 14). A person's *life story* often contains facts that are set in a larger narrative containing many fictive elements, as in the telling of an event that has happened in a person's life (Lauritzen & Jaeger, 1997). The investigator analyzes each life story using a framework that allows for examination of "all requirements of story: setting, characters, [and] action directed toward goals" (Lauritzen & Jaegar, 1997, p. 35). The narrative approach provides the investigator with an organizational structure designed to be responsive to analysis. A typical narrative framework focuses on the "core narrative," or skeleton plot, through four categories (Mishler, 1986), as follows:

1. *Orientation*: describes the setting and character
2. *Abstract*: summarizes the events or incidents of the story
3. *Complicating action*: offers an evaluative commentary on events, conflicts, and themes
4. *Resolution*: describes the outcomes of the story or conflict as the resulting analysis moves toward a reduction of the narration to answer the question, what is the point of this story? (pp. 236-241)

Linden Labs refers to the Second Life platform as "the leader of compelling, cost-effective virtual education solutions to amplify an existing curriculum or create new models for engaged, collaborative learning" (Crease, et al., 2011). On the corporate Web site, there are several references to sectors of their application in which business, nonprofits, educators, and entrepreneurs can develop a virtual presence. The sector of second life designated for use in education is the portion that this study deals with specifically, with the stated goal of "to enhance current education, provide access to users world-wide, [and] to create an open, trusting virtual environment to support the learning process" (Livingston, et al., 2008).

Narrative Analysis

Humans, by nature, are storytellers; "the world as we know it is a set of stories that must be chosen among in order for us to live life in a process of continual re-creation" (Fisher, 1987, p. 5). Coffey and Atkinson (1996) made it clear that they do not make a distinction between narratives and stories.

Lauritzen and Jaegar (1997) analyzed different life stories using a framework that allowed them to examine all requirements of the story — elements such as setting, characters, and actions directed toward goals. According to Boje (1999), stories can be used to train others to achieve, affiliate, and exercise power. Academics and researchers have far too quickly dismissed the need to study stories (p. 1).

Boje, et al. (2004) describes language as being content and context as well, which he describes as as a way to recontextualize content. Recontextualize is simply looking at not only the content or description in the narrative, but to also examine the context to relook at the way the context sets the narrative. “We do not just report and describe with language; we also create with it. And what we create in language ‘uses us’ in that it provides a point of view (a context) within which we ‘know’ reality and orient our actions” (p. 571). This idea is central to analyzing the grand narratives that relate to this research, since context is a vital factor in building trust. Using Boje’s guidelines (2001), one can seek to understand grand narratives, versus the microstoria in the antenarratives. Boje states that “in the interplay between grand and local narrative we can begin to recognize hegemony and posit the dynamics of the relationship.” Furthermore, Boje states that “local microstoria themselves constitute a deconstruction of the grand narrative” (p. 35).

Furthermore, Trochim (2006) makes an important distinction. Qualitative designs are usually better-suited to research studies that aim to investigate complex and sensitive issues in depth in order to generate very detailed information. Quantitative research, conversely, is better-suited to summarizing large amounts of data with the aim of formulating generalizations based on statistical projections. Trochim (2006) summarizes the use of the former, asserting that qualitative research excels at “telling the story” from the participant's viewpoint, providing the rich descriptive detail that sets quantitative results into their human context.

Method and Research Design

The research method and design for this study describe the educator’s experiences with building trust in the virtual-world environment. Trust building allows the educator to create an environment that nurtures learning. The formulation of the method and research design thus considers the following theme questions:

1. What is the educator's experience in building trust in virtual teams?

2. How did the educator know that trust had been built?

3. What similarities and differences exist in building trust in Virtual worlds?

4. What was the effect of on the learning process of building trust in a virtual world?

A small pilot study was conducted to identify the time requirements needed for the interview. The mean time needed to conduct the interview was 42 minutes. The combined log of all interviews and chats for this study is included in Appendix C. All quotes included in this analysis were left in their original forms, including misspellings and text abbreviations, to capture the true essence of the communication exchange; names, however, have been replaced to protect the anonymity and confidentiality of the participants. The investigator used open-ended questions, supporting Creswell's (1998) argument that "phenomenological study emphasizes the meaning of an experience for a number of individuals" (pp. 55–56). Data on how people act and react to phenomena were collected through interviews, which came from open-ended questions posed by the investigator. From the data, the investigator then interrelated the categories of information and wrote a detailed narrative analysis in order to present a deeper understanding.

Population and participants. The total population of Second Life is estimated at approximately one million members worldwide (Lacy, 2012). The participants in this study were volunteers who have used Second Life and are affiliated with education in some capacity, either formally or informally; they were drawn from the pool of educators participating in in Second Life, as defined by available Second Life statistics (Creswell, 2009; Shepard, 2012). This population was considered desirable because of this study's focus on education-related research, and because the participants already had access to Second Life. These factors can be assumed because the sample was drawn from various sources specifically to ensure these requirements.

Second Life was started in 2003, and, as discussed earlier, the purpose of SL is different from that of other MUVEs in that it is primarily used as a virtual social space, in which users explore various worlds and cultures and connect with others from around the world (Malaby, 2009). The official count of higher education institutions in Second Life is not precise; however, tallying the number of post-secondary institutions listed in the SL Education Directory, and comparing that number to a list generated by the search feature, identified over 300 educational institutions. Jennings and Collins (2007) have pioneered this formula in their Second Life research on higher education institutions. The final total indicates that there were approximately 315 post-secondary institutions in world as of June 2012. Creswell (2012) has suggested that an investigator select 5–25 interviews based on several visits to the field to collect interview data in order to saturate the category. For the current study, a total of 24 participants signed up on the initial Web site, hosted on surveymonley.com. However, only 10 people from that Web site survey ultimately participated. Another two people participated directly via Second Life contact, for a total of 12 participants.

Survey Title Sort	Created Sort	Modified Sort	Design	Collect	Analyze Sort		Actions
Participate in SL Research Study	September 7, 2012 2:42 PM	86 days ago				24	Clear Transfer Delete

Table 3.1 – Survey Monkey Report on Participants

Sample. The educators represented many countries, although the majority were in the United States. The investigator had chosen Second Life as the object of study because of its thriving educational communities, with many institutions from which to draw. Participants had to be 18 years of age or older, which was specified in the solicitation for participants in Appendix B.

Respondent Data. The following is a demographic breakdown of the participants in this study. As this figure reveals, 24 respondents signed up to participate in the study. The sampling was thus representative of several international inputs. The investigator conducted all interviews. Transcriptions were a combination of investigator notes from the voice chats and text chat logs. The transcripts were saved as text files as well as to a Word document for purposes of content analysis. Several weeks of discussion transcripts were read immediately following each meeting, and then again multiple times to identify the emergent themes (Lindlof, 1995) that ultimately guided the focus of the analysis.

Within this group, the following countries were represented:

Country	Number of Respondents
United States	12
United Kingdom	3
Greece	3
Ireland	2
Fiji	1
Canada	1
Brazil	1
France	1

Table 3.2 – Respondent Geographic Data

Sampling plan. Another unique feature of gathering research in this instance is that the research is focused on the educators themselves and not necessarily on an institutional setting. The study, as already delineated, was centered on virtual worlds. Volunteer participants were solicited through email invitations sent to people within the education sector of the Second Life resident population. Specifically, participants were taken from two global educational resources — one online and one in Second Life itself. An email was sent from CTUSLResearch@gmail.com to the following email distribution lists: vw-research@utlists.utexas.edu, slrl@list.academ-x.com, and educators@list.secondlife.com. Additionally, a request for participation was also sent to the following groups within Second Life: Real Life Education in Second Life, Second Life Library 2.0, eMax Education, SLL Outreach to Higher Education, Virtual Educators Alliance, UoB Educators, AVALON Educators, LIS Educators in Virtual Worlds, Art and Design Educators, CESL, Educators New to SL, Distance Educators, LCIN SL Educators, the New Media Consortium, and ISTE Educational Technology Association. An online registration Web site (http://www.surveymonkey.com/s/58G6K6C) was then used to log interested participants and gather generic and confidential demographic data to ensure that registrants were over 18 and had experience educating in the SL environment.

Second Life hosts the largest educational presence of any virtual world, involving more than 150 colleges and universities and a very active community of educators that numbers nearly 12,000 (NMC, 2012). This study thus used SL's educational platform to attempt a stratified random sampling, dividing by region the members of this community involved in virtual teams for development, teaching, and/or learning activities that use SL (Trochim, 2002). The sample size of 12 participants proved adequate for this study because it is in keeping with other research in this area (De Jong & Elfring, 2010).

Data collection. A fairly mature history of research exists on trust in face-to-face environments. This prior research was used to create a foundation for this study. This study relied on open-ended questions, interviews, observation, and investigation to see if discernible new patterns would emerge, and to suggest further work in the area (Edmondson and McManus, 2007, p. 1160). This research sought to identify whether any patterns seen in face-to-face environments would also apply to virtual environments.

Dickey (2005) found that the investigator gains greater understanding with the avoidance of tape recordings and word-by-word transcripts. Dickey's argument is that the investigator will glean greater understanding from the extra interviews he or she could conduct in the time it would take him or her to listen to and transcribe a tape recording. Therefore, his suggestion to take keyword notes during the interviews and convert them to themes afterwards was used in the conduct of this study. This methodology was not as time-consuming (or as costly) as producing full transcripts. Therefore, the interviews were collected using keyword notes (see Appendices C and D).

Data collection instruments. Initially, the email solicitation with related registration questionnaire served as the primary instrument. It contained requests for the volunteer's profile information, including generic demographic data and technology access questions. Specifically, it contained questions regarding education experience in Second Life, as well as age eligibility. It also contained a consent form for voluntary participation (see Appendix B).

The registration questionnaire was available through a public Web-based survey site hosted at http://www.surveymonkey.com/s/58G6K6C. Interested participants from the solicitation sources mentioned above were asked to complete the questionnaire and indicate their participation time and date preference. The Web-based survey site also collected all the responses in a data repository. After completing the questionnaire, participants received an email with a link to the Second Life location for the interview and a proposed time slot in which the interview would take place (see Appendix C). Participants were encouraged to participate in the interviews via SL, but were also be given the option of participating via other communication methods such as via email and filling out the questions through text in a survey type format, consisting of the main study questions.

Semi-structured interviewing was the main instrument used in this study as a way to collect data as well as to gain knowledge from individuals. Kvale (1996, p. 14) has described interviews as "an interchange of views between two or more people on a topic of mutual interest, [that] sees the centrality of human interaction for knowledge production, and emphasizes the social situatedness of research data." Semi-structured interviews are non-standardized and are frequently used in qualitative analysis, as they do not test a specific hypothesis (David & Sutton, 2004, p. 87). A list of central themes, issues, and questions to be covered was used, and the order of the questions was changed depending on the direction of the interview. Corbetta's (2003) semi-structured interviews were used, which left the order in which the various topics were dealt with and the wording of the questions to the interviewer's discretion. Within each topic, the interviewer conducted the conversation as appropriate, asking the questions using whatever wording was considered best, giving explanations and asking for clarification if the answer was not clear, to prompt the respondent to elucidate further if necessary, and to establish a style of conversation.

More questions were asked as the conversations evolved, and some questions that arose had not been anticipated at the beginning of the interview. Instant messaging captured typed content, while the investigator gathered keyword notes from any audio used. This type of interview gave the investigator opportunities to probe the views and opinions of the interviewee. Probing is a way for the interview to explore new paths which were not initially considered (Gray, 2004, p. 217). Having the key themes and sub-questions in advance gave the investigator a sense of order from which to draw questions from unplanned encounters (David & Sutton, 2004, p. 87).

The researcher conducting semi-structured interviews is freer than one conducting a structured interview (Kajornboon, 2004, p. 75) in which the interviewer has to adhere to a detailed interview guide. Patton (2002) recommends that the interviewer "explore, probe, and ask questions that will elucidate and illuminate that particular subject . . . to build a conversation within a particular subject area, to word questions spontaneously, and to establish a conversational style but with the focus on a particular subject that has been predetermined." (p. 343).

Dickey (2005) made the point that by avoiding taking notes during interviews and not using a tape recorder, rapport developed more rapidly and effectively between interviewer and subject. However, this requires an excellent memory system on the part of the interviewer that allows him or her to memorize up to 20 distinct themes (more, if necessary) and recall them in order. Thus, instant messages and recordings were also used to collect interview data.

Interview process. As part of the interview process, the investigator encouraged the participants to add feedback in order to enhance the value of the research and the data gathered. The interviewer's objective was to listen to everything the participant had to say and pay particular attention to what the participant did not say and, in the process, build a certain trust with the participant. The investigator's interview responses were based on the work of Haney and Leibsohn (2001):

1. *Opening and closing responses*. These were rehearsed and practiced, and opening and closing statements were purposefully used to set the tone of the interview.

2. *Attending*. This meant giving undivided attention to what the participant was saying and paying attention to what the interviewer saw and heard rather than what she knew.

3. *Empathizing*. By responding to the participant's feelings, the interviewer indicated that he/she was listening. This emotional response showed how the interviewer might feel in the participant's shoes.

4. *Paraphrasing.* Participants were responded to in ways that restated the essence of what they had just said. Paraphrasing not only helped the interviewer (investigator) to clarify understanding of what had just been said, but also helped the interviewee (participant) explore the subject even more deeply.

5. *Giving feedback.* This consisted of responding to the participant, stating what the interviewer had just observed.

6. *Clarifying.* This involved asking the participant to be more concrete or specific.

7. *Directing.* As required, the interviewer would give a specific direction, or go back over what had just been said.

8. *Questioning.* Questions were asked to clarify a meaning or interpretation and/or to encourage the participant to explain something at a deeper level. Questioning was a way to probe.

9. *Playing a hunch.* This included such things as saying, "This is more important to you than you seem to be indicating."

10. *Noting a theme.* Ongoing themes or patterns were noted across interviews.

11. *Noting a discrepancy.* In this situation, the interviewer presented two things that do not seem to fit with each other.

12. *Noting a connection.* The interviewer presented two things that seem to be connected in order to solicit a further response.

13. *Reframing.* The interviewer stated an alternative way of viewing something to help the participant explore the matter more profoundly

14. *Allowing silence.* Responding this way gave the participant time to process and consider the matter at hand more deeply. Silence was also used as a probe.

15. *Self-disclosing*. Sharing some personal information with the participant was sometimes helpful.

The overall purpose of the interview process was to (a) acknowledge the participant's experience; (b) encourage the participant to explore the issue further; (c) allow the participant to ponder; and (d) allow for better understanding of the participant's thoughts, ideas, and behavior. Due to the semi-structured interviewing process, and the objective of getting the educator's story, the interviews were limited to the core research questions, and restricted to periods of no more than two hours.

After recording the data from five participants via a text based survey sent via email, the investigator felt that a follow-up interview with these subjects would be beneficial. Therefore, another interview with two of the participants, who took part voluntarily, used the following set of questions:

1. How would you describe building trust in a virtual environment?
2. What are your perceptions of how your development of trust evolved?
3. Describe your experience with building trust in virtual worlds.
4. What have been the outcomes from building trust in virtual teams as an educator?

Validity. To determine whether the findings were accurate from the standpoint of the researcher, the participant, or readers of the account, the investigator used the Creswell (2003) approach as a procedural process to check the accuracy of the findings (pp. 173-175):

1. Triangulate different data sources of information while examining evidence from the sources and use it to build coherent justification for themes.
2. Use member checking to determine the accuracy of the qualitative findings, take the final report back to the participants, and determine whether these participants feel that they are accurate.
3. Use rich, thick description to convey the findings.

4. Clarify the bias the investigator brings to the study.

5. Spend time in the field so the investigator gains a clear understanding of the phenomenon.

6. Use peer debriefing to enhance the accuracy of the account.

7. Use an external auditor to review the entire project.

The investigator integrated the seven preceding items to test the validity of the work done in this study. This ensured that the study would not come to reflect only the investigator's point of view, but would also encompass the views of the participants, and ensured that the theory drawn from the interviews was consistent with the themes and phenomena of the study.

Reliability. As noted by several researchers, validity does not carry the same connotations in a qualitative study as it does in quantitative research, nor is it a companion of reliability. In a limited way, qualitative researchers can use reliability to check for consistent patterns of theme development among investigators. Overall, reliability plays a minor role in qualitative inquiry (Creswell, 2003).

Specific process of data collection. The investigator collected data through detailed interviews and instant messages in which the participants shared, via stories, their experiences of teaching within SL. This study used a qualitative research design as a way to understand and investigate the *meaning* attributed to a social or human problem. This process entailed *emerging* questions and procedures, and data collection was conducted in the participants' Second Life setting. The data was then evaluated *inductively*, going from specific to broad themes, and interpreted.

Most communication during the interviews took place using the text chat in the tool in Second Life. When possible, voice chat was used to augment the instant messages; often, however, the audio feature was not used because of a time lag in sending and receiving of message, which resulted in frustratingly slow communication between the two parties. All text chats were stored in files that were used for narrative analysis. Appendix C captures all this information.

The investigator's role. The investigator assumed the role of interviewer–observer, spending substantial time within SL as a student, instructor, and doctoral candidate conducting research. However, before a discussion of the results of this study, one must understand the role of the investigator as a participant-observer; this is relevant to this section, since it pertains to the validity of the study. Relationships were formed over time and with active involvement in the community of study. These relationships were often lasting ones, enduring for weeks, months, or even years. It was through this active social involvement that the investigator was able to identify the gatekeepers and key informants within the culture, and solicit their participation in this study. In line with other qualitative studies of this type, Lindlof (1995) described the role of participant-as-observer as that of an investigator who "enters a field setting with an openly acknowledged investigative purpose, but is able to study from the vantage point of one or more positions within the membership" (p. 144).

Benefits. This study does not offer any direct benefits to its participants. However, this study hopes to provide a foundation to help educators identify ways in which a collaborative learning environment can be established through trust, in which the participants of this study can learn by doing. In other words, by telling their stories of how they have built trust, they will be gaining a better understanding of what they do, and how they do it, so that they can be cognizant and apply these techniques in their classrooms. As Dickey (2005) cited, benefits of this kind of study design include being able to experiment without concern for real-world repercussions and being able to learn by doing, while Ondrejka (as cited in Eschenbrenner et al., 2008) mentioned a greater level of comfort in asking questions and an ability to develop a sense of shared learning. Conway (as cited in Eschenbrenner et al., 2008) also noted that the virtual environment could provide opportunities to introduce more creativity into the classroom.

Assumptions. Because this study used descriptive experiences, it is qualitative in nature and did not use hypotheses. However, it did make three assumptions:

1. Each of the participants would have the ability to express his or her thoughts and ideas about trust and virtual worlds.

2. The investigator would be able to interpret the data without unduly projecting biases. In qualitative research, one realizes and acknowledges biases while at the same time trying to minimize their effects on the research findings.

3. The committee members would be aware of and knowledgeable about the sample selection and data collection processes used for this study.

Ethical consideration. There are challenges to using a qualitative method. Richardson (2000) has observed that qualitative research is not as straightforward as authors represent it to be. Authors choose evidence selectively, clean up subjects' statements, unconsciously adapt metaphors, and bore readers. The ethical challenge for this study involves the investigator's representations of the subjects, the authority the investigator had to interpret the subjects' lives and the writers' voice, and the ethnography used to complete the study (pp. 923-948).

Furthermore, as with any research project involving human subjects, institutional review board (IRB) approval was a critical part of the process. Approval for the request for volunteers was also obtained from the moderators of the email distribution lists and SL groups to ensure that it was appropriate to use these lists for solicitation. The interview questions for this research were also put through the university's IRB approval process to ensure that the interviews met university and federal guidelines for the protection of participants. Further permission was collected from the participants in the form of the required "informed consent" formula and a detailed permission form (see Appendix A). Since this study was conducted within the virtual world of Second Life, the informed consent form was also delivered via a notecard to each participating avatar. The subject then sent the investigator an instant message, which served as the subject's signature with the date of consent, if the subject had not already submitted consent via the survey tool.

Human subject protection. It was imperative that a detailed permission form be obtained from each participant before he or she was allowed to participate in the study. The informed consent form is attached as Appendix A. The purpose of this form was to provide the participant with information about the research so that he or she could make an informed decision about participation.

According to Linden Lab (2012), the Second Life client login uses password-only authentication over secure HTTP. At no time does Linden Lab have access to any user's passwords. Passwords, and any information entered through the "My Account" page on the Second Life Web site, are encrypted, and use a secure HTTP connection. Additionally, the Second Life Viewer provides a connection to Second Life that does not compromise a computer's security. At this time, there is no known remote exploit to the client. The viewer also uses a Vivox-plugin for spatial and group voice chat, which is quality checked and provided exclusively by Linden Lab. The viewer does not use any other third-party plugins, nor is there currently a plugin architecture. The private SL region of Acheron was used for interviewing the participants. This area was set-up as part of an estate in the Second Life world. These regions provide a highly manageable environment for conducting private business in the virtual world of Second Life. A region owner may choose to exercise full control over access to private regions in the estate. The region's administrative tools enable its owner (and designated managers) to create an access list, by individual or group, ensuring that only approved users can enter the region. This makes a private region such as Acheron secure from eavesdropping. The region is surrounded by an equivalent void space, represented by water; void space cannot be crossed by walking, running, flying, or by camera. There is currently no Linden Scripting Language (LSL) script, which could listen to instant messages, voice communication, or media streams, nor can an LSL script directly capture visual content such as objects or textures (Linden Lab, 2012).

As noted above, the informed consent form was delivered to each participant's avatar via a notecard. Notecards are simple text documents that one can create and share in Second Life. The two participants who had not signed the informed consent form in the survey responded by digitally signing the notecards and returning them to the investigator's avatar. These served as the participants' acceptance and signature of the informed consent form. Second Life secures notecards from unauthorized access, use or disclosure. Therefore, the personally identifiable information the subjects provided via computer was stored on servers in a controlled, secure environment. Any personal information (such as a name, age, etc.) transmitted is protected through the use of encryption, such as the Secure Socket Layer (SSL) protocol. This is true for both the notecards in SL and the surveys collected through Survey Monkey, the online tool used for the initial survey. The instant messages were securely stored on the investigator's external hard drive. This drive will then be secured in a safe for the requisite three-year period, at the end of which time the data will be securely wiped.

Although no study is completely risk-free, the investigator could not identify any harm or distress risks posed to those participating in this research. Each participant was informed that if he or she became uncomfortable, he or she could cease participation at any time. Furthermore, the investigator will contact participants and the dissertation committee if the investigator receives any new information that could change a subject's decision to participate in this study. When the results of the research study are published, the names or identities of the participants will not be revealed. All information collected is strictly confidential.

Participation in this study was voluntary. If a person chose not to participate, or a subject chose to withdraw from the study, there were no consequences for him or her.

Specific process for data analysis. The investigator analyzed the data recursively to identify emerging themes and topics of interest. Then the investigator referenced and revisited notes and artifacts to assess the utility of the original theoretical framework for interpreting the data with a thematic analysis. The investigator attempted constantly to assess and ensure the credibility and verifiability of the interpretations of the data, in order to increase the reliability of this research.

The investigator first looked at the data by type, then organized the data by theme by doing a Boje (2001) theme analysis. Boje (2006) defines theme analysis as a dialectical decoding and re-coding process that presents a holistic graphic image of the theme fan-and-branch process. Further, in his text *Narrative Methods for*

Organizational and Communication Research (2001), he describes how theme analysis looks at the deductive, inductive, etic and emic categories, which can then be expanded upon by taking an antenarrative approach (p. 122). The investigator applied the theme and sub-theme analysis of narrative types (Yolles, 2007) and then moved on to an antenarrative analysis with the data, as discussed in detail in the next chapter.

Chapter IV: Analysis and Results

Analysis of the data has resulted in the identification of the following emerging themes in the stories: educators' embrace of Virtual worlds; students' experiences with SL; relevance; respect for differences; working to build a trust experience; communication; knowledge of students' understanding; learning and seeing the immersive creativity; and using different teaching modalities. These all contribute to the facilitation of trust in a virtual education environment. This chapter will describe in detail how these results were formed from the analysis.

The participants' responses to questions regarding trust in the virtual world were quite varied. All 12 participants were over 18 and had experience with teaching in virtual worlds. Not all participants provided information on the kind of institution at which they taught, or what they taught; among those who did provide some of this information, however, there were participants from both elementary (pre-K-12) and higher education institutions. Participants also represented both various regions of the US and several other countries, as described in the data collection section. This study allowed participants to express their own views of their experiences, and their definitions of building trust and meaning in the collaborative learning environment. The investigator, however, did present each participant with the study definitions of the terms presented in chapter one so that each could answer the interview questions with more clarity.

The rationale for selecting a smaller sample size was to get in-depth information through lengthy and sequential interviews that would yield large quantities of data. The sample size of 12 participants proved adequate for this study because it was in keeping with other research in the area (De Jong & Elfring, 2010) and is appropriate to a qualitative research design (Creswell, 2009). The educators who participated in this study are summarized in the table below. Those who participated via the survey tool or by email are signified by S, whereas those who were interviewed are coded with P. As stated above, 10 participants used the survey tool to sign up for the study, while another two participated directly through Second Life.

	Started	Mins	Code		Country	School	Grade Level	Time in SL
1	10/5/12 12:12AM	3			Greece	University of the Aegean	Higher Ed	YEARS
2	10/5/12 1:55PM	2		P5	USA	East Carolina University	ALL	5
3	11/13/12 1:08PM	14			Ireland			4
4	11/13/12 1:31PM	2			USA	Indiana U Northwest	Higher Ed	5
5	11/13/12 2:27PM	3			USA	DePaul University	Higher Ed	5
6	11/13/12 2:52PM	1			USA	Cheyney U	Higher Ed	
7	11/13/12 5:02PM	4			France			
8	11/14/12 3:28AM	3	S6		Brazil	Federal U of Parana	Higher Ed	6
9	11/14/12 8:19AM	3			Canada	U of Calgary	Higher Ed	
10	11/15/12 12:19PM	2			USA	Indiana U Northwest	Higher Ed	1
11	11/19/12 7:58AM	3			USA	Cheyney University	Higher Ed	4
12	12/07/12 9:45AM	1			UK	U of the West of England	Higher Ed	4
13	1/15/13 9:48AM	11	S5		USA	Penn State	Higher Ed	6
14	1/15/13 10:46AM	25			Ireland	Computer Education Society		6
15	1/15/13 2:34PM	37		P4	USA			5
16	1/15/13 5:16PM	1			Fiji			5
17	1/16/13 2:10AM	4			Greece			
18	1/16/13 9:03AM	57	S4	P3	USA	Alternative Youth Activities	9th-12th	4
19	1/16/13 9:43AM	40		P2	UK	RM Education	ALL	6
20	1/17/13 5:15AM	2			UK	U of the West of England	Higher Ed	
21	1/17/13 7:11AM	7	S3	P1	USA	East Carolina University	Higher Ed	7
22	1/18/13 10:41AM	4			Greece	U of the Aegean	Higher Ed	
23	2/4/13 2:48PM	3	S2		USA	US Navy	Higher Ed	
24	2/4/13 10:29AM	33	S1		USA	Phoenix Charter School	Pre-K - 12th	
SL1	1/20/13 8:27AM	20		P6	Taiwan	Tainan Arts University	Higher Ed	5
SL2	11/16/12 8:42AM	32		P7	Greece	University of the Aegean	Higher Ed	7

Table 4.1 – Responses to Solicitation

Utilizing Boje's methods for narrative and communication research, the rest of this chapter details the activities that were conducted to support a qualitative narrative analysis of educators' stories. The following sections display the combining of these data elements in a holistic manner, which allows the blending of sections from Boje's narrative analysis model. To identify the portions of the data used for analysis, superscripts are used to map back to the data in Appendix C.

Context. Many of the participants stated that they were willing to participate in this environment in much the same way that they would participate in education contexts in real life.[4E,8G,10G,11FG] This, however, was not the case for everyone. Some did not want to interact with an avatar, for example, because they did not know who the people behind the avatars were.[9F,12G,13G] When looking at the use of a virtual world as a classroom platform, one has to consider such issues that may arise with these environments. For example, if students experience frustration due to a lack of proper tools (technology) or experience (ease of navigation), a teacher may lose them right at the start.[17H] Another challenge is the computer illiterate student who is not easily able to access or operate in this environment.[10F,11G] Many educators came into Second Life with a certain level of "buy in," yet many participants said that they still experienced anxiety and frustration. These feelings were amplified for those with less comfort in virtual environments, and with those students, any buy-in could quickly be obliterated.[3B,10F] A big part of creating a trusting environment is creating familiar surroundings in which people are comfortable.[10F,11F] For many, this can mean construction of areas in which their avatars can sit, stand, and otherwise move in extremely humanistic ways.[4D,10F] In this study, however, there were also many people who were comfortable flying around, or vaporizing into thin air and then reappearing on the other side of the island.[110J] There were users who did not even have humanistic avatars, but rather showed up as characters such as Big Bird or a werewolf.[8G,10G] All of these factors played into the educators' comfort levels (and trust) with operating in a virtual world.[3B,11F] This deconstruction analysis thus provided the insight that, right from the start, some people have greater comfort and trust levels in virtual worlds than do others.

Grand Narrative

The grand narratives for the interview environment can be defined as the multiples of stories present in a virtual world, as each person will bring his or her own interpretation to the scene. When analyzing the discourses, it is thus important to consider which ones support the grand narrative, which ones marginalize the other discourses, and why. Therefore, in this phase of the analysis, looking at the collective storytelling system as a whole, in which the telling of stories is a key part of identifying the educators' sense-making, is critical for identifying the grand narrative. Allowing for this flexible interpretation, the educators' stories can be put into a "big picture" context to allow for exploration of how themes of building trust evolved over time and across multiple accounts. To allow for the different story accounts, the stories were collected over a five-month period (see Appendix C). Additionally, those surveys which were not in-depth were followed up at a later time with interviews (as shown in Table 4.1). The building of trust by educators in virtual worlds is therefore seen as a storytelling system in which the educators collectively look at their past, present, and future perceptions to make sense of the events. Consequently, the building of trust involves not just one story, but as multiples of stories, multiples of voice, and multiples of story interpretations, which both resist and accept one another (similarities and differences among stories).

Microstoria Analysis

Microstories are the portions of the grand narrative that call into question the big picture by collecting the accounts of "little people", or those stories that wouldn't be heard in the grand narrative. It is impossible to detail the myriad of microstories available in this environment. Virtual worlds like Second Life reference and respond to the real world in many ways. All of the microstories we see in the ethnographic portrait of a society in real life are thus present in virtual life as well.[15H,17H,19H] There are real relationships in Second Life that have ramifications in the real world.[4E,8G,9F,10G,11FG,12G,13G] These stories can give us a brief glimpse into historical causation on the level of small groups in which most of real life takes place, and open that history to people who would be excluded by other methods.

For example, a few years ago a heated debate was in full force concerning the use of virtual worlds in education contexts. This debate was fueled with the critics contending that there was a lack of professionalism and protection in this use of virtual worlds. Such critics essentially argue that they know what the "little people" want, or rather what they need, better than do the people themselves. They believe it is their duty to protect these people from themselves. Yet, as identified in the grand narrative analysis, both extremes — one that focuses only on the success stories of Second Life (as the official brochure and case studies do) and one that tells only negative stories of the SL experience (such as many blogs and critics do) — are both examples of very narrow ways in which to analyze the organizational narrative of trust in Second Life.

Network Analysis

After one has identified the dualities, grand narrative, and microstories, it is vital to conduct a network analysis through which to discuss the relationships in this study. The analysis process was enhanced through the use of NVivo 10.

Text preparation began with the importation of all artifacts into NVivo, a proven software program used for qualitative analysis. Since NVivo is designed to handle rich-text-based information, in which deep levels of structure analysis are required, it automates the processes of classifying, sorting, and arranging information, enabling the exploration of trends. Due to the vast amounts of data collected in this study, NVivo was used to analyze, classify, sort, and arrange data automatically. Coding the text involved categorizing particular text segments. NVivo thus added to the transparency of the data analysis and allowed for the creation of numerous active links in the texts. Also, models were used to provide a diagrammatic overview of the relationships between nodes. The exhibit below shows the screens that appear in NVivo at the coding stage. This program was also used to examine the coded text in its context, embedded in its place in the original document (see Appendix E).

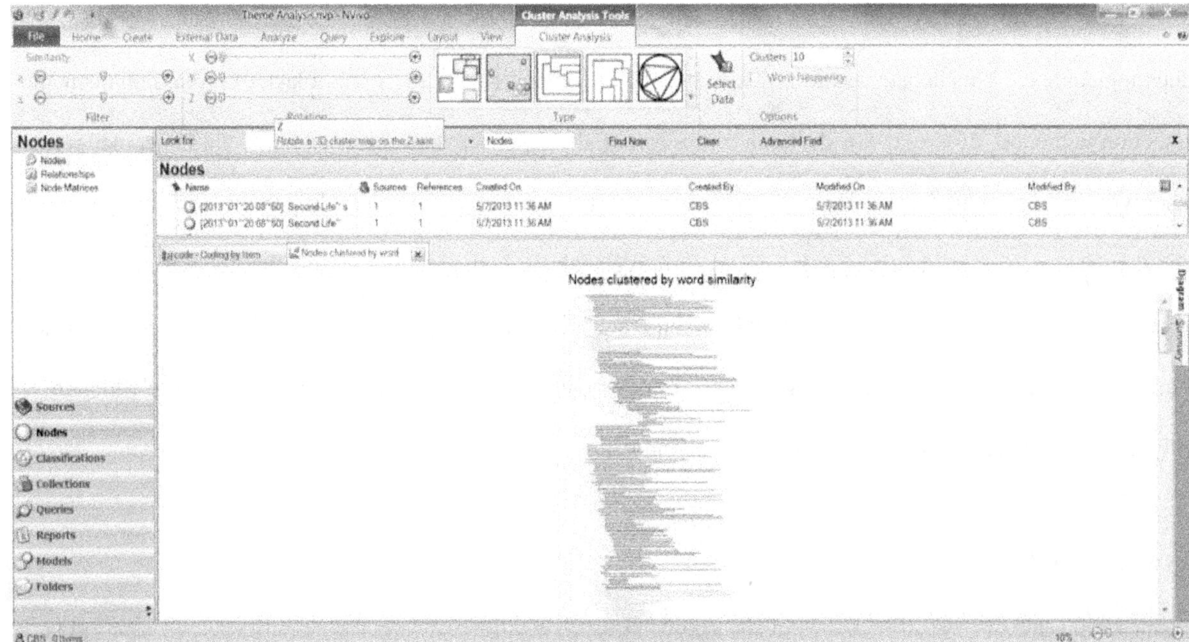

Figure 4.2 – Screenshot of NVivo Software and Nodes

The story fragments can then be organized into narrative maps, which read as nodes and relationships (links) for abstract model building. This portion of the analysis seeks to understand the complex dynamics of storytelling among people across their social networks. Furthermore, with this method, the stories can be depicted as links to names, places, or other nodes. To begin this process the data was categorized into respondent data, survey data, and interview data (see Appendix C). From this a keyword list was made using NVivo (see Appendix D), and coding, with this list as a guide, was done to identify the stories as links.

In the following sections, stories as links are used as a way to analyze the various ways that the stories relate to each other. The virtual world of Second Life is a web of storytelling organizations. Yet, many of these stories are in conflict with each other and do not fit the universal tale of virtual worlds used for learning. These stories use a plurality of stories, voices, and realities, as well as a multiplicity of ways to interpret stories, and exhibit the infinite play of differences in meanings mediated through socially constructed practices. However, some stories are more hegemonic than others, and thus will marginalize the other discourses when looked at as a whole. In this case, the story fragments were categorized into narrative maps, which read as nodes and relationships (links) in the figure below (see Appendix G for full graphic):

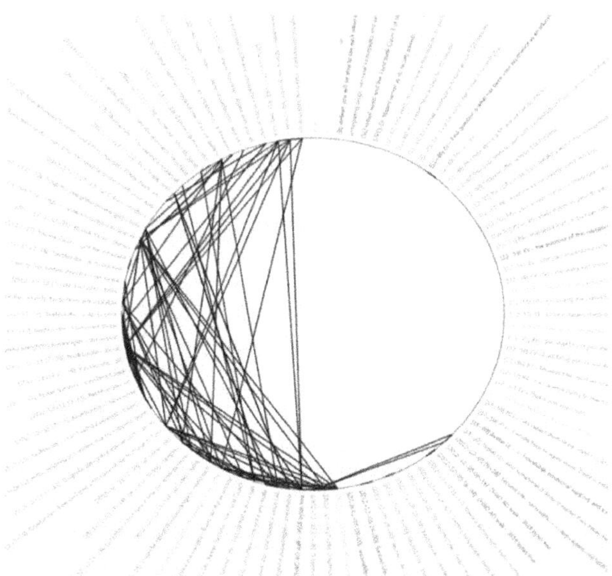

Figure 4.3 - Story Fragments as Links in Network Mapping

These interactions can be traced to reveal the patterns of relationship among educators and the other nodes, linking the stories and voices. Additionally, a relationship exists among the educators, student and other residents, and these influence each other. Second Life is just one storytelling organization in a large web of interrelated parts. Due to the nature of the environment, several possible links exist which are influenced by the other stories in the mix. It is thus necessary to consider this as a multi-stranded, embedded, and dynamic system in order to understand some of the links among the various groups. Finally, the network mapping helps to display the architecture in a way that allows us to see how the stories and relationships are intertextually linked to each other. From this networking, a dialectical decoding and re-coding process emerges, to render a holistic graphic image of the theme fan-and-branch process, which can then be expanded by taking an antenarrative approach.

Intertextuality Analysis

Intertextuality considers each text as a network of fragments that refer to and interrelate with other narrative texts. This section explores how the intertextual system and networking theory of trust can be extended to virtual educational environments. In its simplest form, grouping the data according to keywords, count, weight, and similar terms can identify intertextuality, as shown in Appendix D. Based on the data gathered in this study, the intertextual aspects of the interviews were analyzed by examining the links between educators and their perceptions of student trust, interpretations in the network of relationships among the educators' stories. There is an ongoing dynamic textual production process, of which each utterance and the text itself is a moment. As an examples, keyword notes and intertextual elements are identified (see Appendix C):

learning	Links to	acquisition, check, checked, condition, conditions, hear, hearing, instructions, know, knowledge, learn, learned, learning, learns, read, see, seeing, sees, studies, study, take, takes, taking, teach, teaching, watch, watching
see	Links to	attend, attended, attending, catch, check, checked, consider, considering, control, date, encounter, experience, experiences, fancy, find, finding, findings, look, looking, looks, meet, meeting, meetings, project, projects, realize, regarding, see, seeing, sees, view, visit, visiting, visual, watch, watching
get	Links to	arriving, becomes, becoming, begin, begins, bring, bringing, brings, catch, come, comes, develop, developed, development, find, finding, findings, generates, get, getting, going, having, incur, incurs, let, lets, letting, make, makes, making, received, start, started, stimulate, take, takes, taking
trust	Links to	believe, commitments, committed, hope, hopefully, hoping, hopes, sure, trust, trusted, trustfulness, trusting
work	Links to	act, bring, bringing, brings, exercise, exercises, form, functioning, functions, going, influence, make, makes, making, play, played, playful, playing, process, run, shape, shapes, studies, study, turn, work, worked, working, works

Table 4.4 – Example of Intertextual Elements

Hegemony is defined by the *Fontana Dictionary of Modern Thought* as a means of

> political and economic control exercised by a dominant class, and its success in projecting its own way of seeing the world, human and social relationships as common sense and part of the natural order by those who are, in fact, subordinated to it. (Lawrie, 1999)

Hegemonic assumptions about teaching have caused great harm to educators' attempts to build trust: the irony of hegemony is that educators take pride in acting on the very assumptions that work to enslave them. This was evident in such educators' statements as, "From my experience it [trust] should've appeared even before students' introduction inside a VW"[13G] and "It's all about trust from the real world."[13G]

When these statements were followed up with questions about how would educators build trust if they have no face-to-face relationship with students, the reply was, "They (virtual trust) are involved simultaneously with the trust of real life, I cannot separate both of them (face-to-face and virtual)"[13G]; "This is easy for me. I was the first. I did everything on my own. The only person to trust was me"[6E]; and "I have had limited success with building trust in the virtual world but have been able to physically meet with my students and then build an in-world relationship from that."[3A] All of these views came from educators who felt that there is only one way to educate, and that is face-to-face; they were unwilling or unable to break this mold to see that they were in fact limiting themselves with this subordination to hegemony because of their experience.[12G]

Causality Analysis

As is evident by this stage of the analysis, stories are living things. They are woven together in complex relationships. To further understanding of how trust is built by educators in virtual worlds, and build a richly detailed description of the process, this phase of the analysis examined how educators' stories are laced with causal assertions — "'A' happened, so 'B' must be the cause." This type of analysis is structuralist, which consists of identifying through content analysis the causal assertions in the data set of narrative texts. Then the approach outlined in Rubin &

Rubin (2005) was used to code the data. This involved examining the interviews and looking again at the literature to gain ideas on what themes and concepts to note, and to develop new concepts where appropriate, and then to work out the definitions prior to doing the causal analysis (p. 221) (see Appendices E and F).

In this phase of the analysis, the interviews and transcripts were analyzed to capture the utterances for various types of causal assertions. These words were then highlighted with different colors to represent an emergent typology. The typology was then assessed according to how the assertions clustered by theme or types. Each text was marked as representing generative, psychological, or successionist causality (and each sub-type as necessary — contributory, sufficient, remote or illusory correlation, psychological essentialism, etc.). Any antenarrating of causality was noted, and new types of causality were identified. Therefore, based on the causal relationships and coding, a keyword list was created to identify the types of cause as exampled below (see Appendix D).

The codes for trust-defining factors were extracted from the typology of the stories presented (Appendix E). It was then possible to look at the generative causality narratives to identify prior events that are connected to and cause subsequent events, in order to get the context of the causality.

Sufficient cause can produce an effect by itself. For example, the transcripts from the study illustrate the effect that "virtual teams are more engaged,"[10F] caused by the fact that "since they can't see each other in RL they are more open and honest."[11F] This assertion posits that being open and honest causes engagement.

Necessary cause must be present for the effect to occur, but by itself cannot produce the effect. For example, one educator stated that "I build trust by being honest and being who I am and laughing when necessary, and telling them if I know it and if don't know it. Being friendly, open, and not being bothered if I don't know something. In other words, being genuine."[8F] All of these factors are necessary for trust to occur, but are not by themselves the cause of trust in virtual education environments.

Contributory cause may lead to an effect, but cannot produce it by itself. For example, the level of dexterity a user has with a virtual world platform could be seen as a contributory cause. As one participant said, "Yes, that is what makes me angry about some educators: they come here [to SL] to teach and never learn how to really use the platform. They call themselves experts and they can barely sit in a chair. It's very frustrating . . . I think that would definitely decrease my trust if I were their student."[10F] This knowledge is contributory, but not sufficient or necessary in itself to cause distrust.

Proximate cause means that various events happen close to the effect, but without being sufficient, necessary, or contributory causes. While virtual worlds are proximate to MOOCs, MMOGs, and games, none of those things is a sufficient, necessary, or contributory cause of trust or learning in virtual worlds.[10F,311K]

Remote cause happens distant from an effect. It occurs when the mechanism linking two events has not been specified. For instance, in other remote learning tools that can work with Second Life, "We are working to develop more resources for . . . remote learning and distance education. We want to be able to develop teleconference means to support on-line approaches; for instance, it is [currently] difficult for their (meaning students) personalities to show through in the SL avatar form."[6D] These are remote causes of possible distrust in SL, and do not have necessary or a sufficient causal connections to trust.

Chaos cause suggests that effects emerge from initial conditions, but the patterns vary from starting points. A given event may have any of a number of effects. Rather than the linear argument that A results in B, the effects can be non-linear or completely unpredictable. Consider this educator's statement:

> I haven't thought about it, trust is a huge part of it, because people don't know me. In Moodle and other non-3-D environments, it is about safety and they know me, from the language lab and my teaching English. In virtual worlds, where there is no face-to-face relationship, they come to the class and then come back and have built that relationship. They either like your style and what you are teaching or they don't come back. There are several students that I have that come to class religiously every week and won't miss it. If they are going to miss they let me know. They have no obligation to choose me, but they do.[8F]

This shows that the educator's style of teaching, whether in real life or virtual, had the unanticipated result of trust.

Plot Analysis

Relevant to this study is the definition of plot as the events that connect the previous analysis and the chaining of cause and effect into a pattern or structure. Plot is not just a chronology of events; it is what links events together in a narrative structure.

Ricoeur's account of the way in which narrative represents the human world is termed *emplotment*, indicating that which brings the diverse elements of a situation into an imaginative order, in just the same way as does the plot of a story. Emplotment configures events, agents, and objects, and renders those individual elements meaningful as part of a larger whole in which each takes a place in the network that constitutes the narrative's response to why, how, who, where, when, etc. Strategies and changes to the interpersonal dynamics of trust in virtual worlds are always being emploted by the collective of educators. As many institutions are turning to alternative means of delivering distance education, these educators have to adapt to the new technologies and, in many ways, the new teaching styles that accompany this dynamic medium[virtual worlds].[17H] The traditional lecture style of teaching is not effective in a medium like Second Life, which shifts the plot into a revolution of change.[7F,10F,15H,105J] Besides the idealistic plot of trust in no different in virtual worlds, there is some techno futurist material in the transcripts, meaning the focus on future possibilities of technology. For example, some educators talked about advanced technology, which they believe was more effective for distance education.[19H] Such technology, however, requires investment, training, and a shift in the face-to-face relationships between educators and students.[6A,7F,12F] There is a shift as well in the educators' narratives from stories of authority and hierarchy to a more futurist (a person who engages in identifying possible futures with technology) narrative, with a positivist orientation toward educators as facilitators, or toward the concept of a flipped classroom.[2A,7F,9F,9G,10F,14H,18H,19H] In this study, both these genres (traditional and non-traditional) emerged, and the pure narrative (original or founding) is present in the transcripts as well. This is evident in the stories of "leaders emerg[ing]",[2E] and "working with teams in different school systems"[1A] to "resemble the trust you can initiate in a face-to-face encounter".[1A] Yet also present are the strategies for "transferring innovative knowledge"[7G] by showing "respect [for] each member — [for] his [or her] thoughts or opinions — as a unique (cyber-) entity, and in this notion I follow a trail that consists [of] the possible opportunities of collaboration and anticipated learning outcomes that . . . [emerges] from this process."[13G]

What results from this analysis is that we see a move away from more than the traditional and individualistic institutional constructs driven by a single emplotment. Rather there are competing and rapidly changing strategic discourses, and there are parallel storylines. Educating in virtual worlds is an example of the use of polyphonic strategies, of bits and pieces of strategies and polyphonic strategy-making.[7-10FG,14-19H] No single plot, emplotment, or storyline unfolded in this virtual network.

Theme Analysis

Theme analysis is an examination of dialect, coding and re-coding to get a holistic image of the theme fan-and-branch process (see Appendix E).

Boje discusses ways of using both deductive and inductive approaches, as well as a mixture of insider categories ("emic") and outsider categories ("etic") that are more appropriate for gaining a deeper understanding of the focus of the study. This study used a deductive approach to collect the themes and categorize them based on based on some degree of similarity among the themes. Accordingly, etic taxonomy refers to the categories from the viewpoint of the outsider observing others' worlds (Boje, 2001: 122-124).

The paradigm is shown visually in the table below:

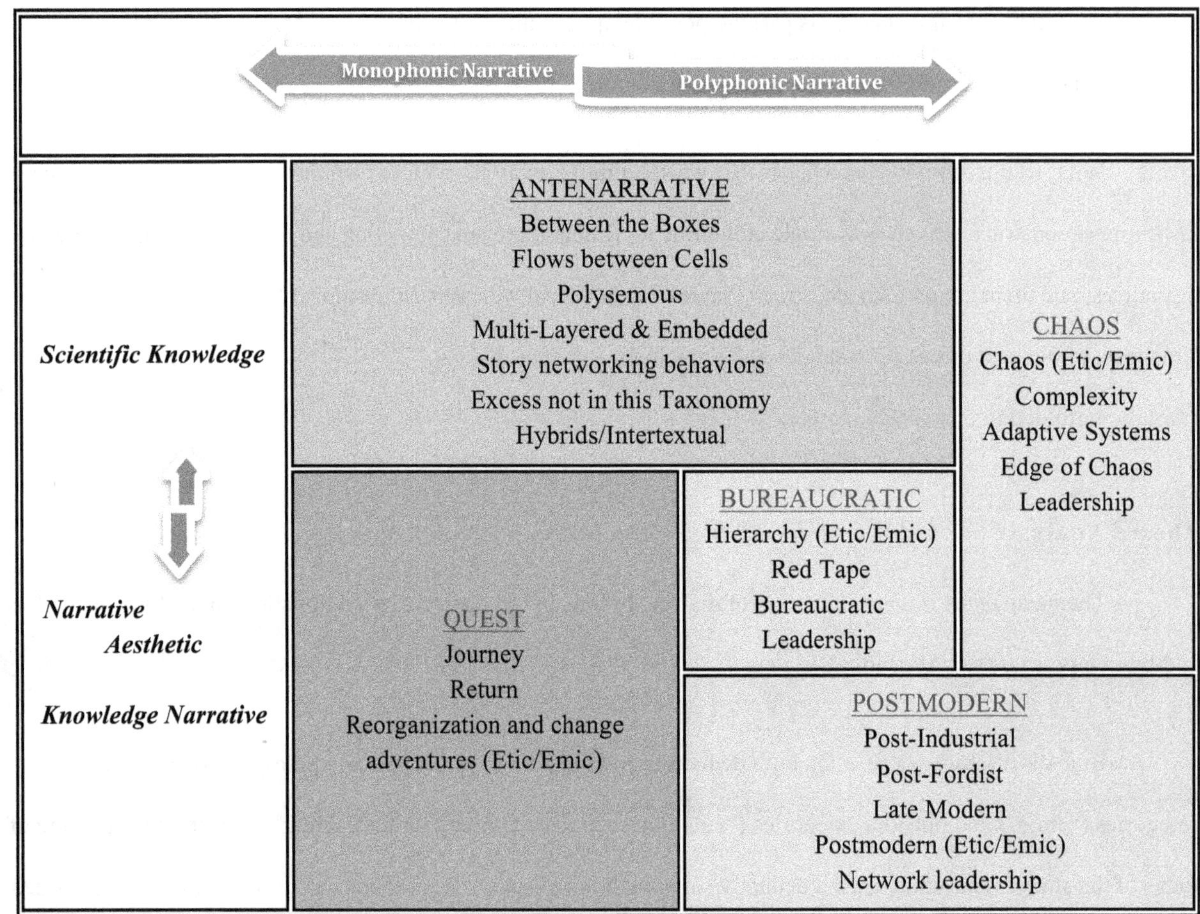

Table 4.5 - Interactive Narrative Types (adapted from David M. Boje)

In using the above table to search and annotate the location of various quotations in relation to each of the themes, a paradigm emerged. Once the taxonomy of themes and their similarities and differences was mapped, an antenarrative approach was taken. Accordingly, the antenarrative analysis was concerned with "what gets left out of the themes and taxonomy cages and what goes on between cells" (Boje, 2001: 124-125). Boje has thus argued against taxonomy and has instead looked to the trace stories to see how story themes are embedded contextually in folds and refolds (2001: 126). The following examples illustrate this technique.

In the following story as told by Franetovic (2012): *In virtual worlds the majority of students were familiar with a paradigm where the instructor is always right* (Bureaucratic). *During the exercise where students evaluated the instructor's example RPG narrative, a familiar dynamic emerged* (Post-Modern & Quest). *Namely, a few students challenged the instructor when critiquing her narrative* (Quest & Chaos). *However, this was not something she appeared accustomed to* (Bureaucratic & Antenarrative). *Students received a slight push back from the instructor, which reaffirmed the status quo in which she was unquestionably right* (Bureaucratic & Quest). *The interaction transpired despite the fact that the students made valid points* (Post-Modern, Antenarrative & Chaos). *This very small, however noteworthy incident demonstrated that though openness, equality, and collaboration had been encouraged, the authentic learning environment was challenging to adhere to in the way it had been introduced, and to some extent, implemented* (Antenarrative). *It was difficult to foresee the students entirely changing their incoming behaviors to adopt new ones, if the instructor herself had doubts or difficulties with the authentic learning environment, for example, the equalizing of the playing field when she was being critiqued* (Chaos, Quest & Antenarrative).

From this analysis, a paradigm taxonomy emerges in which the narrative themes interact in such a way as to see how the educator's bureaucratic context is challenged by the student's quest context, folding the story into a chaos and antenarrative context to show that even though the taxonomy of openness, equality, and collaboration were present, that the traditional and bureaucratic taxonomy was challenging a dynamic interaction and was resisting adaptation and change.

The next story comes from the Bromley College of Further and Higher Education. In Barry Spencer's experience with teaching an object-oriented programming course, he observed that *Second Life is offering a steep change in social learning environments* (Chaos, Quest & Antenarrative). He asserted *that the unique qualities of 3-D virtual worlds can provide opportunities for rich sensory immersive experiences, authentic contexts and activities for experiential learning, simulation and role-play, modeling of complex scenarios, a platform for data visualization and opportunities for collaboration and co-creation that cannot be easily experienced using other platforms* (Post-Modern, Antenarrative & Chaos). Spencer believed that *access to this different way of conceptualizing a problem, together with the ability of students to interact with one another online, promoted improved engagement* (Quest & Post-Modern). He compared the communication tools of a typical virtual learning environment (VLE) to those offered in multi-user environments such as Second Life. In a VLE, he suggested *that the individual learner remains essentially alone, whereas in Second Life, synchronous communication, identity, and voice combine to offer another level of virtual learning* (Bureaucratic & Chaos). His story shows paradigm taxonomy illustrates in what way the institution at which he teaches is meeting the challenge of how to harness learning opportunities for its students using virtual worlds. The project also included end-of-course student surveys to help evaluate the learner experience of this use of Second Life (JISC RSC, 2009).[15H]

These stories serve to highlight many of the themes present in the antenarratives of education in Second Life. However, two themes emerged as particularly pervasive. First was the theme of using virtual worlds such as Second Life as a "test-bed" for real life applications.[12F,15H,19H,60K] This was one of the most common themes present in several of the antenarratives regarding why people enjoyed using this application. They could take great risk in the virtual environment to model and see how a project might play out with very little real world risk. This gave them confidence and experience.

Another key theme that is significant to the concept of trust in learning is the ability of the virtual world construct to enable collaboration across geographical boundaries.[6C,12F] Not only is this an important theme for virtual teams of students and educators. but it also creates a worldwide community of knowledge. We can easily collaborate with our instructors, peers, and counterparts, share lessons learned, and assist in research. This suggests that this open and co-creative environment encourages learning at a higher level than the traditional modalities.

In virtual worlds, educators are suspended in a complex web of storied relationships that change and move across time and space in resistance to opposing narratives and that combine to reveal the complex storytelling dynamics of how to build trust in virtual worlds used for education. These stories serve to highlight many of the themes present in the antenarratives of education in Second Life. As depicted in the word-frequency visual below, shared sayings and themes emerged in the subjects' responses. These themes serve to provide insight into the thoughts of the educators as they told their stories. Several occurrences of words such as "team," "groups," "cooperation," "experience," and "members" emphasized the significance and dependency of trust in group collaboration, while the high frequency of words such as “fun,” “challenging,” “entertaining,” “work,” and “different” offered potential insights into the usefulness of this emerging technology and its potential capabilities in education (see Appendix D).

Figure 4.6: Word Cloud on Responses

Summary

The results and findings from the detailed analysis reviewed in this chapter show that the major themes emerging in the stories that contribute to the facilitation of trust in a virtual education environment include:

- The educator’s level of embracement of virtual worlds for teaching
- The students’ experience and familiarity with virtual worlds (like SL)
- The relevance of the topic
- The respect for differences
- Working to build a trusting experience
- Communication
- Knowledge of students’ understanding and catering to those needs
- Learning and seeing the immersive creativity
- Using different teaching modalities

The following table captures how these findings relate back to the research questions.

What is the educator's experience in building trust in virtual teams?	Themes emerged from educators from all over, at all instruction levels, and with different levels of experience. The common themes were that: 1) the ease with which trust it built varies based on student familiarity with VWs; 2) the ease with which trust is built varies based on educators' resistance to or acceptance of VWs; 3) students are more participative, open, and honest with the protection of an avatar; 4) building trust takes time and patience.	1A, 2A, 3A, 4A, 5A, 6A, 7F, 8F, 8G, 9F, 4D, 4E, 10F, 11F, 15H, 19H, 154J, 221J, 251J, 317J
How did the educator know that trust had been built?	Communicated effectively, and felt able to present concerns, ideas, and suggestions for improvement, as well as to handle misunderstandings. They [the students] continue to work together. They felt comfortable making mistakes and sharing them. Commitments were made, and follow-up happens. People were prompt and attentive — more dynamically active. Students were engaged, laughing and learning. Educators freely shared plans, projects, outcomes, the good and the bad, and shared ideas including cooperative learning experiences.	1B, 2B, 3B, 4B, 5B, 6B, 7F, 7G, 8F, 8G, 9F, 4D, 4E, 10F, 11F, 15H, 19H
What similarities and differences exist in building trust in Virtual worlds?	The spectrum here runs from the extremes of trust must be built with a face-to-face relationship first and then extended into the VW to the extreme of it is easier to build trust virtually, because there is no risk, and they often learn better, and these relationships spill over into real life, and everything in between, very little similarity existed in the core themes.	1C, 2C, 3C, 4C, 5C, 6C, 7F, 8F, 8G, 9F, 4D, 4E, 10F, 11F, 15H, 19H
What was the effect on learning of building trust in a virtual world?	The process of building trust met the needs of learners; presented an opportunity to expand educational opportunities; and provided a model for others. There was the ability to laugh and play around yet help students to refocus when necessary. The process fostered a collaborative environment that nurtures creativity in my students. It built a neutral place in which students compared, contrasted, shared, discussed, and exchanged ideas and thoughts. Students could interact effectively with faculty and vice-versa to create a cohesive learning environment.	1D, 2D, 3D, 4D, 5D, 6D, 7F, 8F, 8G, 9F, 4D, 4E, 10F, 11F, 15H, 19H

Table 4.7 – Results to Research Question Mapping

Overall, it is apparent that this technology can be used for distance learning applications, and that the facilitation of trust is key to using it successfully. Virtual worlds are an immersive and engaging environment. They stimulate systematic thinking and discussion of the real challenges that face our world and our society, and in particular, of how emerging technologies might be applied to solve them. This study served to explore this topic in more depth. Ultimately, a deeper understanding of how to create a trusting environment in which everyone is willing to participate and share ideas, interact, and collaborate has been achieved.

Chapter V: Implications and Future Research

The focus of this dissertation was on increasing the understanding of the dynamic nature of trust in virtual environments by examining the stories of educators who have had experience in building trust in the virtual classroom. The study identified the themes in educators' perception of the role of trust in virtual classrooms. The study served to identify the similarities and differences among different educators' stories. From this, the research explores the concept of a learning environment and how social capital can influence an educator's success or failure in facilitating learning experiences in virtual worlds. Virtual worlds rely on emerging technologies to facilitate coordination, communication, and control in the environment, and those technologies can shape the way trust develops within a team (e.g. Jarvenpaa et al., 1998; Jarvenpaa & Leidner, 1999; Hung, et al., 2004; Peters & Manz, 2007). This research has argued that virtual worlds offer unique capabilities that have the potential to affect the development of trust and learning. The offering of a rich medium and providing support for 3-D visual representations of objects and people (Owens et al., 2010) provides for an immersive experience (Cooper, 2009). While this study has served to find the generalized themes that are evident in the narratives of virtual educators, the scope of this study was limited. This section addresses the implications of this research and the significance of the study's findings. Additionally, this chapter addresses future research suggestions.

Implications

This study provides much-needed empirical evidence on the significance of trust in virtual education environments used to facilitate learning. The practical significance of this study is to futurists, investigators, instructional designers, and educators. Furthermore, for parties interested in understanding how trust building affects learning outcomes in virtual environments, this study offers a foundation for further research and brings together new and important implications for immersive virtual environments. For example, design science is actively researching this technology, and engaging in the creation of technological artifacts that have an impact on people and organizations. However, the focus in virtual world applications is usually on problem-solving, indicating an overly simplified view of the contexts in which designed artifacts must function. These must be combined with behavioral and organizational theories to develop an understanding of problems, contexts, solutions, and evaluation approaches adequate to serve the academic research and practitioner communities (Boje, 2009; Hevner et al., 2004). The findings offer potential for leveraging the power of a virtual 3-D environment in order to build trust in collaborative education. While virtual worlds, including Second Life, are cited as a "shared creativity tool" or "creativity space" (Hindman, 2011) which can support collaborative education, further studies could review the findings here to see if they can be applied to other virtual worlds used for learning, or to other collaborative learning tools from other perspectives (such as students).

Suggested Research

As the scope of this study was limited, there still exists a significant need for further research in this area. One such area is that of the relationship of trust to engagement and learning, and the interaction among these three variables. Prior research has suggested that the more trust there is between students and educators, the more engaged the student becomes, and increased learning was subsequently reflected in achievement scores (Cooper, 2009). Future research is needed to see if higher levels of trust correlate positively to higher levels of achievement.

Additionally, prior research has suggested that technological issues have a significant impact on learner interest. New technologies will need to be integrated into education to engage and immerse students and support the learning experience. The quality of the experience when using immersive media is a key factor in the design and development of instruction approaches (Jones, 1998). Additionally, current literature on the emerging media of immersive learning environments suggests that technological complexity is an inherent factor in virtual worlds (Hayes, 2006, Helmer & Light, 2007; Cooper, 2009). Future learners will enter classrooms already accustomed to virtual worlds through their experiences with online gaming. These students are innovative, social thinkers and will demand that their educators do more than relay knowledge through traditional lectures (Oblinger & Oblinger, 2005; Cooper, 2009).

The results of this research are limited to the virtual world of Second Life and to identifying themes of trust using narrative analysis techniques. The generalization of this study is limited to similar virtual educational environments, with similar audience scope, measures, and interview constructs. Additionally, while a representative sample was sought for the educator interviews, the true total population of educators in Second Life is not known.

Furthermore, this study did not explore the perspectives of the students using the virtual platform, but rather focused only on the stories of educators. I point to the responsibility of educators and leaders to create a trusting environment. This poses a question regarding the responsibility of other VW participants, such as students, in the facilitation of trust. How do students show that they trust educators, as well as fellow students? Further research could be fruitfully conducted from the point of view of students to identify the themes in their stories, and to see if they confirm or deny the authority of the hegemonic voice of the "educator."

There are several criticisms leveled at the use of virtual worlds as platforms for learning, the main one relating to accessibility. To use these environments, students' computer access must meet certain technological standards. Further research could examine stories from the perspective of people who do not have access to such technology and are therefore at a disadvantage. Smith-Robbins (2011) points out that the traditional classroom lecture is inferior to generalizing to all learning modalities, but economic constraints and stretched faculty are hard-pressed to innovate when already overloaded. The initial enthusiasm around Virtual worlds may have been a symptom of a need for solutions to these difficult problems. Virtual worlds were seen as a possible solution to a lack of resources, just as e-books, iPads, laptop programs, and other technologies have been treated as a panacea for what ails much of higher education. Regardless, however, of whether or not these virtual environments more broadly used, studies on how to maintain high quality education with smaller budgets should continue. A single technology will not solve all issues. However, the intention behind the enthusiasm for such tools may help us think more deeply about what we are hoping to change and how we can go about it. Virtual worlds may not turn out to be as broadly relevant in education as many had hoped, but that underlying hope is still very relevant.

Conclusion

This empirical qualitative study examined a topic of significant interest. The findings of this study offer a greater understanding of the underlying themes and elements that contribute to building trust as a means to facilitate education and learning outcomes. Though the emerging media of virtual worlds is powerfully immersive and engaging, the quality of the instructional content and the design are significant factors in facilitating the most effective learning outcomes. A high level of trust among students in these environments has been suggested to improve learning outcomes, but further research in this area is needed. The results of this study add to the literature on virtual worlds, trust, the use of emerging technology, and virtual education. This analysis supports the current research on social capital by showing that educators have found that interaction in the medium of Second Life is advantageous in fostering an active learning community. These communities are described as creative, cohesive, exciting, and diverse (De Maggio, et al., 2009; De Vaan, et al. 2011). Showing how educators can motivate learning by encouraging the increased use of virtual worlds provides evidence of the pedagogy of virtual learning environments, and their usefulness in exploring fragmented, polyvocal, polysemous, and polydiscursive learning stories. The practical significance of this study speaks to futurists, researchers, instructional designers, and educators. Furthermore, parties interested in understanding how trust-building affects learning outcomes in virtual environments may also find this study useful. This study offers a foundation for further research, and brings together new and important implications for immersive virtual environments. Design science, for example, is actively researching this technology, and engaging in the creation of technological artifacts, which have impact on people and organizations; however, the focus is usually on problem-solving, offering too narrow a view of the contexts in which designed artifacts must function. These must be combined with behavioral and organizational theories to develop an understanding of problems, contexts, solutions, and evaluation approaches adequate to serve the academic research and practitioner communities (Hevner, et al., 2004).

As the scope of this study was limited, there still exists a significant need for further research in this area. Consistent methods of conducting virtual research in the context of education need to be refined. Specifically, virtual behavior biases needs to be explored. This recognizes that the population of virtual worlds differs from that of the real world, and acknowledges the possibility that individuals behave differently online. It is yet unclear how individuals' judgment and decision-making processes differ when mediated through emerging technologies. For example, there is some initial evidence that social distance is negatively associated with reciprocity (e.g. Charness, Haruvy and Sonsino, 2007), but there remain other aspects of virtual association that are yet unexplored. Better understanding of the interpersonal dimensions of these differences would provide enhanced context for additional research to address these areas. Another such area is that of the relationship of trust to engagement and learning, and the interaction among these three variables. Prior research has suggested that the more trust there is between student and educator, the more engaged the student is, and increased learning may subsequently be reflected in achievement scores (Cooper, 2009). Future research is needed to see if the data suggests that higher levels of trust correlate positively to higher levels of achievement.

Determining what factors are involved in building trust in virtual education means that these factors can then be leveraged to facilitate collaborative learning, resulting in a high level of positive group outcomes, loyalty, and commitment to fellow students. Academic interest in the potential of 3-D immersive environments for teaching and learning is profoundly evident (Cooper 2009), and empirical exploration is warranted. This qualitative study examined a topic of significant interest. The findings of this study clarify the underlying themes and elements that contribute to building trust as a means of facilitating education and learning outcomes. Though the emerging media of virtual worlds are powerfully immersive and engaging, the quality of the instructional content and the design are still significant factors in facilitating the most effective learning outcomes. Trust in these environments has been suggested to improve the learning outcomes, but further research in this area is needed. This study could benefit comparable environments or studies in related research environments or with a similar design. Findings from this qualitative study provide insights for educators, instructional designers, trainers, and administrators considering the use of a virtual world environment for learning. The primary aim of this study was to get a holistic view of trust in virtual worlds that use storytelling. The descriptions, inferences, and critical reflections in this study might influence best practices in emerging and future instructional methods, and in virtual world integration in higher education institutions and beyond.

References

Adler, P., & Kwon, S. (2002). Social capital: Prospects for a new concept. *Academy of Management Review, 27*, 17–40.

Agar, M. (2005). Telling it like you think it might be: Narrative linguistic anthropology, and the complex organization. *E:CO Issue, 7*(3–4), 23–34.

Air Education and Training Command. (2008). *On learning: The future of air force education and training.* Retrieved from http://www.au.af.mil/au/awc/awcgate/aetc/afd-080130-066.pdf

Akdere, M., & Conceicão, S. (2006). Integration of human resource development and adult education theories and practices: Implications for organizational learning. In F. M. Nafukho & H.-C. Chen (Eds.), *Referred proceedings of the AHRD 2006 International Conference* (pp. 295–301). Bowling Green, OH: Academy of Human Resource Development.

Alavi, M. and Yoo, Y. (1997). Is Learning in Virtual Teams Real? *Working Paper Harvard Business School*, Boston, MA.

Allen, M. (Ed.). (2007). *The next generation of corporate universities: innovative approaches for developing people and expanding organizational capabilities*. Pfeiffer.

Allen, E., & Seaman, J. (2007). Online Nation. Five Years of Growth in Online Learning. New York: The Sloan Consortium, 31. ERIC, EBSCOhost.

Ball State University. (2011). *Emerging media initiative.* Retrieved from https://sitecorecms.bsu.edu/Academics/CentersandInstitutes/EmergingMedia/Videos/EMintro.aspx

Bell, M. W. (2008). Toward a definition of "virtual worlds." *Journal of Virtual Worlds Research, 1*(1), 1-5.

Bellman, K., & Landauer, C. (2000). Playing in the mud: Virtual worlds are real places. *Applied Artificial Intelligence, 14*(1), 93–123. doi:10.1080/088395100117179

Bendoly, E., Thomas, D., & Capra, M. (2010). Multilevel social dynamics considerations for project management decision makers: Antecedents and implications of group member tie development. *Decision Sciences, 41*(3), 459–496. Retrieved from ABI/INFORM Global. Document ID: 2115363901.

Benford, S., Greenhalgh, C., Rodden, T., & Pycock, J. (2001). Collaborative virtual environments. *Communications of the ACM, 44*(7), 79–85.

Boellstorff, T. (2008). *Coming of age in Second Life.* Princeton, NJ: Princeton University Press.

Beollstroff, T. (2010). Culture of the cloud. *Journal of Virtual Worlds Research, 2*(5), 3-9.

Beranek, P., & Martz, B. (2005). Making virtual teams more effective: Improving relational links. *Team Performance Management, 11*, 200–213.

Boje, D. M. (1991). Consulting and change in the storytelling organisation. *Journal of Organisational Change Management, 4*(3), 7–17.

Boje, D. M. (1994). Organizational storytelling: The struggles of pre-modern, modern and postmodern organizational learning discourses. *Management Learning, 25*(3), 433-461.

Boje, D. M. (1995, August). Stories of the storytelling organization: A postmodern analysis of Disney as "Tamara-Land." *Academy of Management Journal, 38*(4), 997-1035.

Boje, D. M. (1999). *Storytelling leaders*. Retrieved from http://business.nmsu.edu/~dboje/leaders.html

Boje, D. M. (2001). *Narrative methods for organizational and communication research.* London, England: Sage.

Boje, D. M., Rosile, G. A., & Gardner, C. L. (2004, August). Antenarratives, narratives and anaemic stories. In *paper for the All Academy Symposium Actionable Knowledge as the Power to Narrate, New Orleans: New Orleans meeting of the Academy of Management* (Vol. 9).

Boje, D. M. (2007). Globalization antenarratives. In A. Mills, J. C. Helms-Mills, & C. Forshaw (Eds.), *Organizational behavior in a global context* (pp. 505–549). Toronto, ON: Garamond Press.

Boje, D. M. (2011a). *Shaping the future of storytelling in organizations: An antenarrative handbook.* London: Routledge.

Boje, D. M. (2011b). *Storytelling and the future of organizations.* New York: Routledge Taylor & Francis.

Boje, D. M., Oswick, C., & Ford, J. D. (2004). Language and organization: The doing of discourse. *Academy of Management Review, 29*(4), 571–577.

Boland, T. (2009). *Efficacy of the 3-D multi-user virtual environment (MUVE): Second Life for learning in cognitive constructivist and social constructivist activities* (Unpublished doctoral dissertation). Capella University.

Bolton, R., & Saxena-Lyer, S. (2009). Interactive services: A framework, synthesis and research directions. *Journal of Interactive Marketing, 23*, 91–104. doi:10.1016/j.intmar.2008.11.002

Book, B. (2004). *Moving beyond the game: Social virtual worlds.* Paper presented at the State of Play 2 Conference, New York Law School, New York, NY.

Bredo, E., & Feinberg, W. (1982). *Knowledge and values in social and educational research.* Philadelphia: Temple University Press.

Brothers, D. (1995). *Falling backwards: An exploration of trust and self-experience.* New York: Norton .

Cacioppo, J. T., Lorig, T. S., Nusbaum, H. C., & Berntson, G. G. (2004). Social neuroscience: Bridging social and biological systems. In C. Sansone, C. C. Morf, & A. T. Panter (Eds.), *The SAGE handbook of methods in social psychology* (pp. 383-404). Thousand Oaks, CA: Sage Publications.

Calongne, C. (2008, September–October). Educational frontiers: Learning in a virtual world. *Educause Review,* pp. 36–48.

Candle, A. E. (1965). Lab-Line "Tailors" an Environment to your need! *Environmental Quarterly, 11.*

Charness, G., Haruvy, E., & Sonsino, D. (2007). Social distance and reciprocity: An Internet experiment. *Journal of Economic Behavior & Organization, 63*(1), 88-103.

Casalo, L. V., Flavian, C., & Guinaliu, M. (2008). Fundaments of trust management in the development of virtual communities. *Management Research News, 31*, 324–338. doi:10.1108/01409170810865145

Castronova, E. (2001). Virtual worlds: A first-hand account of market and society on the cyberian frontier. *The Gruter Institute working papers on law, economics, and evolutionary biology* (Vol 2). Retrieved from http://www.bepress.com/cgi/viewcontent.cgi?article=1008&context=giwp

Chase, N. (1999). Learning to lead a virtual team. *Quality, 38*(9), 76.

Chen, H. (2006). Flow on the net—detecting Web users' positive affects and their flow states. *Computers in Human Behavior, 22*, 221–233.

Choi, D., Kim, J., & Kim, S. (2007). ERP training with a web-based electronic learning system: The flow theory perspective. *International Journal of Human–Computer Studies, 65*, 223–243. doi:10.1016/j.ijhcs.2006.10.002

Claridge, T. (2004). *Social capital and natural resource management* (Doctoral dissertation, School of Natural and Rural Systems Management, University of Queensland).

Crease, R., Pymm, B., & Hay, L. (2011). Bridging the gap—engaging distance education students in a virtual world. *ascilite Conference* 1, 307-313. Retrieved from: http://www.ascilite.org.au/conferences/hobart11/downloads/papers/Crease-concise.pdf

Coffey, A., Atkinson, P. (1996). *Making sense of qualitative data: Complementary research strategies*. London: Sage.

Cohen, S.G., & Bailey, D.E. (1997). What makes teams work: Group effectiveness research from the shop floor to the executive suite. *Journal of Management, 23*(3), 239-290.

Cohen, S. G., & Gibson, C. B. (2003). In the beginning: Introduction and framework. In C. B. Gibson & S. G. Cohen (Eds.), *Virtual teams that work: Creating conditions for virtual team effectiveness* (pp. 1–13). San Francisco, CA: Jossey- Bass.

Connelly, F. M., & Clandinin, D. J. (1990). Stories of experience and narrative inquiry. *Educational Researcher, 19*(5), 2-14.

Cooper, K. E. (2009). *Go with the flow: Examining the effects of engagement using flow theory and its relationship to achievement and performance in the 3-dimensional virtual learning environment of Second Life* (Unpublished doctoral dissertation). University of Central Florida.

Coppola, N., Hiltz, S. R., & Rotter, N. (2004). Building trust in virtual teams. *IEEE Transactions on Professional Communication, 47*(2), 95–104.

Corbetta, P. (2003). *Social research: Theory, methods and techniques.* London: SAGE Publications.

Coutu, D. L. (1998). Trust in virtual teams. *Harvard Business Review*, 76: 20–21.

Creswell, J. W. (1998). *Qualitative inquiry and research design: Choosing among five traditions.* Thousand Oaks, CA: Sage.

Creswell, J. W. (2003). *Research design: Qualitative, quantitative, and mixed methods approaches* (2nd ed.). Thousand Oaks, CA: Sage.

Creswell, J. W. (2009). *Research design: Qualitative, quantitative, and mixed methods approaches* (3rd ed.). Thousand Oaks, CA: Sage.

Creswell, J. W. (2012). Qualitative inquiry and research design: Choosing among five approaches. SAGE Publications, Incorporated.

Creswell, J. W., & Clark, V. L. P. (2007). *Designing and conducting mixed methods research.* Thousand Oaks, CA: Sage Publications.

Csikszentmihalyi, M. (1975). *Beyond boredom and anxiety.* San Francisco, CA: Jossey-Bass.

Csikszentmihalyi, M. (1990). *Flow: The psychology of optimal experience.* New York, NY: Harper & Row.

Daniel, B., Schwier, R. A., & McCalla, G. (2003). Social capital in virtual learning communities and distributed communities of practice. *Canadian Journal of Learning and Technology/La revue canadienne de l'apprentissage et de la technologie, 29*(3).

David, M. & Sutton C.D. (2004). *Social research: The basics.* London: SAGE Publications.

Davidson, S. (2008). An immersive perspective on the Second Life virtual world. *Computer and Internet Lawyer, 25*(3), 1–16. Retrieved from ProQuest Computing. Document ID: 1436136101.

Davis, A., Murphy, J., Owens, D., Khazanchi, D., & Zigurs, I. (2009). Avatars, people, and virtual worlds: Foundations for research in metaverses. *Journal of the Association for Information Systems, 10*(2), 90–117. Retrieved from Business Source Premier database.

De Jong, B. A., & Elfring, T. (2010). How does trust affect the performance of ongoing teams? The mediating role of reflexivity, monitoring, and effort. *Academy of Management Journal, 53*, 535–549.

De Maggio, M., Gloor, P. A., & Passiante, G. (2009). Collaborative innovation networks, virtual communities and geographical clustering. *International Journal of Innovation and Regional Development, 1*(4), 387-404.

Denzin, N. K. (1989). *Interpretive biography.* London: Sage Publications.

Denzin, N. K., & Lincoln, Y. S. (Eds.). (2011). *The SAGE handbook of qualitative research.* SAGE Publications, Incorporated.

DeSanctis, G. and Poole, M.S. (1997). Transitions in teamwork in new organizational forms. *Advances in Group Processes, 14*, 157-176.

De Vaan, M., Vedres, B., & Stark, D. C. (2011). Disruptive diversity and recurring cohesion: Assembling creative teams in the video game industry, 1979-2009. Retrieved from http://hdl.handle.net/10022/AC:P:13094

Dey, I. (1993). *Qualitative data analysis: A user-friendly guide for social scientists.* London: Routledge.

Dickey, M. D. (2005). Three-dimensional virtual worlds and distance learning: Two case studies of Active Worlds as a medium for distance education. *British Journal of Educational Technology, 36*(3), 439–451.

Dirks, K. T., & Ferrin, D. L. (2001). The role of trust in organizational settings. *Organization Science, 12*, 450–467.

Dolfsma, W., & Dannreuther, C. (2003). Subjects and boundaries: Contesting social capital-based policies. *Journal of Economic Issues, 37*, 405–413.

Dourish, P. (2001). *Where the action is: The foundations of embodied interaction.*Cambridge, MA: MIT Press.

Driscoll, J. W. (1978). Trust and participation in organizational decision making as predictors of satisfaction. *Academy of Management Journal, 21*(1), 44-56.

Duarte, D. L., & Tennant-Snyder, N. (1999). *Mastering virtual teams.* San Francisco: Jossey-Bass.

Du Bois. J. W., Schuetze-Coburn. S., Cumming, S., & Paolino, D. (1993). Outline of discourse transcription. In J. A. Edwards & M. D. Lampert (Eds), *Talking data: Transcription and coding in discourse research* (pp. 45-87). Hillsdale. NJ: Lawrence Erlbaum.

Edmondson, A. C., & McManus, S. E. (2007). Methodological fit in management field research. *Academy of Management Review, 32*(4), 1155–1179.

Elliot, C. (2007). *In a virtual world, how do you build real trust?* Retrieved from http://business.nd.edu/newsandevents/research_news_article.aspx?id=1073

Eschenbrenner, B., Nah, F. F. H., & Siau, K. (2008). 3-D virtual worlds in education: Applications, benefits, issues, and opportunities. *Journal of Database Management (JDM), 19*(4), 91-110.

Fedor, D. B., Ghosh, S., Caldwell, S. D., Maurer, T. J., & Singhal, V. R. (2003). The effects of knowledge management on team members' ratings of project success and impact. *Decision Sciences, 34*(3), 513–559. doi:10.1111/j.1540-5414.2003.02395.x

Field, J. (2005). Social capital and lifelong learning. In *The Encyclopedia of Informal Education.* Retrieved from http://www.infed.org/lifelonglearning/social_capital_and_lifelong_learning.htm

Fisher, W. R. (1987). *Human communication as narration: Toward a philosophy of reason, value, and action.* Columbia, SC: University of South Carolina Press.

Fisher, S.G., Hunter, T.A. and Ketin Macrosson, W.D. (1997). Team or group? Managers' perception of the differences. *Journal of Managerial Psychology, (12)*4, 232-243.

Foley, M., & Edwards, B. (1997). Escape from politics? Social theory and the social capital debate. *American Behavioral Scientist, 40*, 550-561.

Franceschi, K., Lee, R. M., Zanakis, S. H., & Hinds, D. (2009). Engaging group e-learning in virtual worlds. *Journal of Management Information Systems, 26*(1), 73–100. Retrieved from EBSCOhost.

Francovich, C., Reina, M., Reina, D., Dilts, C. (March 2008) Trust Building Online: Virtual Team Collaboration and the Development of Trust. In J. Nemiro, M. Beyerlein, L. Bradley, & S. Beyerlein (Eds). *The handbook of high-performance virtual teams.* San Francisco: Jossey-Bass

Franetovic, M. (2012). *A higher education case: Millennial experience toward learning in a virtual world designed as an authentic learning environment.* (Doctoral dissertation). Retrieved from Proquestion Dissertations and Theses. (Accession Order No. 1010417478)

Friedman, T. L. (1999, November 17). Next, it's E-ducation. *New York Times,* p. A29. Retrieved from http://www.oslerbooks.com/telecom/education.pdf

Gephart, R. P. (1991). Succession, sensemaking, and organizational change: A story of a deviant college president. *Journal of Organizational Change Management, 4*, 35-44.

Gibson, C. B., & Manuel, J. A. (2003). Building trust: Effective multicultural communication processes in virtual teams. In C. B. Gibson & S. G. Cohen (Eds.), *Virtual teams that work: Creating conditions for virtual team effectiveness* (pp. 59–86). San Francisco, CA: Jossey-Bass.

Giddens, A. (1991). *Modernity and self-identity: Self and society in the late modern age.* Palo Alto, CA: Stanford University Press.

Gilbert, B. (2009, June 1). *Virtual worlds market forecast 2009-2015.* Retrieved January 21, 2011, from Strategy Analytics:http://www.strategyanalytics.com/default.aspx?mod=reportabstractviewer&a0=4779

Grant, K. (2008). *Shift in Spiritual Leadership: Analysis of Metanoia Stories to Get at the Spiritual Aspect* (Doctoral dissertation, Regent University).

Gray, D. E. (2004). *Doing research in the real world.* London: SAGE Publications.

Greenberg, P. S., Greenberg, R., & Antonucci, Y. L. (2007). Creating and sustaining trust in virtual teams. *Business Horizons , 50*(4), 325-333.

Griffith, T.L., Sawyer, J.E., & Neale, M.A. (2003). Virtualness and knowledge in teams: Managing the love triangle of organizations, individuals, and information technology. *MIS Quarterly*, 27: 265-287.

Guillet, B. D., & Penfold, P. (2013). Conducting Immersive Research in Second Life: A Hotel Co-Branding Case Study. *International Journal of Hospitality & Tourism Administration, 14*(1), 23-49.

Guo, Y., & Barnes, S. (2007). Why people buy virtual items in virtual worlds with real money. SIGMIS Database, 38(4), 69-76. doi: 10.1145/1314234.1314247

Guru, A., & Nah, F. H. F. (2001). Effect of hypertext and animation on learning.*Managing Internet and Intranet Technologies in Organizations: Challenges and Opportunities*, 50-61.

Hackman, J. R., & Morris, C. G. (1975). A review and proposed integration. In L. Berkowitz (Ed.), *Advances in experimental social psychology* (Vol. 8, pp. 45–99). New York, NY: Academic Press.

Hakonen, M., and Lipponen, J. (2009). It takes two to tango: The close interplay between trust and identification in predicting virtual team effectiveness. *The Journal of eWorking, 3*(1), 17-32.

Haenlein, M., & Kaplan, A. M. (2009). Flagship brand stores within virtual worlds: The impact of virtual store exposure on real-life attitude toward the brand and purchase intent. *Recherche et Applications en Marketing (English Edition), 24*(3), 57–79.

Handy, C. (1995). Trust and the virtual organization. *Harvard Business Review, 73*(3), 40–50.

Haney, J. H., & Leibsohn, J. (2001). *Basic counseling responses in groups: A multimedia learning system for the helping professions.* Brooks/Cole Thomson Learning.

Harty, C., & Whyte, J. (2010). Emerging hybrid practices in construction design work: Role of mixed media. *Journal of Construction Engineering and Management, 136*(4), 468–476. doi:10.1061/ASCECO.1943-7862.0000146

Hayes, E. (2006). *Situated learning in virtual worlds: The learning ecology of Second Life.* Retrieved from http://www.adulterc.org/Proceedings/2006/Proceedings/Hayes.pdf

Helmer, J., & Light, L. (2007). Second Life and Virtual Worlds. *Learning Light Limited.* Retrieved from http://www.norfolkelearningforum.co.uk/wp-content/uploads/2009/04/virtual-worlds_ll_oct_2007.pdf

Hevner, A. R., March, S. T., Park, J., & Ram, S. (2004). Design science in information systems research. *MIS Quarterly*, *28*(1), 75-105.

Heudin, J. (2000). *Virtual worlds: Second International Conference, VW 2000.* [Paris, France]Springer-Verlag.

Hicks, D., Lisanti, M., Doolittle, P., Friedman, A., Hartshorne, R., Swan, K. (2009). Integrating technology into the social studies classroom. In K. Cennamo, J. Ross, & P. Ertmer (Eds.), *Technology integration for meaningful classroom use: A standards-based approach* (pp. 409–424). Belmont, CA: Wadsworth.

Hof, R. D. (2006, April 30). My Virtual Life. *Bloomberg BusinessWeek*. Retrieved from http://www.businessweek.com/magazine/content/06_18/b3982001.htm

Hoffman, D. L., & Novak, T. P. (1996). Marketing in hypermedia computer-mediated environments: Conceptual foundations. *Journal of Marketing, 60*, 50–68.

Hoffman, D. L., & Novak, T. P. (2009), Flow online: Lessons learned and future prospects. *Journal of Interactive Marketing, 23*(1), 23–34.

Hung, Y. T., Dennis, A. R., & Robert, L. (2004, January). Trust in virtual teams: Towards an integrative model of trust formation. In *System Sciences, 2004. Proceedings of the 37th Annual Hawaii International Conference on* (pp. 11-pp). IEEE.

Jarvenpaa, S. L., Knoll, K., & Leidner, D. E. (1998). Is anybody out there? Antecedents of trust in global virtual teams. *Journal of Management Information Systems, 14*, 29–64.

Jarvenpaa, S., & Leidner, D. (1999). Communication and trust in global virtual teams. *Organization Science, 10*(6), 791–815. Retrieved from Business Source Premier database.

Jarvenpaa, S. L., Shaw, T. R., & Staples, D. S. (2004). Toward contextualized theories of trust: The role of trust in global virtual teams. *Information Systems Research, 15*, 250–267.

Jelen, M., & Orel, M. (2010). *Second Life as a learning environment.* Retrieved from http://www.slideshare.net/MarkoOrel/second-life-as-a-learning-environment-presentation

Jenkins, H. (2006). *Convergence culture: Where old and new media collide.* New York: New York University Press.

Jenkins, H. (2011). *Introduction to communications technologies.* Retrieved from http:/henryjenkins.org/2011/01/introduction_to_communications.html

Jennings, N., & Collins, C. (2007). Virtual or virtually U: Educational institutions in Second Life. *International Journal of Social Sciences*, *2*(3), 180-186.

Jin, S. A., & Lee, K. M. (2010). The influence of regulatory fit and interactivity on brand satisfaction and trust in e-health marketing inside 3-D virtual worlds (Second Life). *CyberPsychology, Behavior & Social Networking, 13*(6), 673-680.

JISC RSC (Regional Support Centres), (2009). Bromley College: Teaching real-life software development skills in a multi-user virtual environment (Second Life). Retrieved from http://www.excellencegateway.org.uk/page.aspx?o=240765

Jones, M. G. (1998). *Creating electronic learning environments: Games, flow and the user interface.* Paper presented at the National Convention of the Association for Education Communications and Technology, Houston, TX.

Kajornboon, A. B. (2004). *Creating Useful Knowledge: A Case Study of Policy Development in E-learning at Chulalongkorn University Language Institute*(Doctoral dissertation, University of Melbourne, Faculty of Education).

Kanawattanachai, P., & Yoo, Y. (2002). Dynamic nature of trust in virtual teams. *Journal of Strategic Information Systems*, 11, 187–213. Retrieved from http://sprouts.aisnet.org/2-10

Kaplan, A., & Haenlein, M. (2009). The fairyland of Second Life: Virtual social worlds and how to use them. *Business Horizons, 52*(6), 563–572. doi:10.1016/j.bushor.2009.07.002.

Katzenbach, J.R and Smith, D.K. (1993). *The wisdom of teams: Creating the high-performance organization.* Boston, MA: Harvard Business School Press.

Kemp, J., & Livingstone, D. (2006, August). Putting a Second Life "metaverse" skin on learning management systems. In Proceedings of the Second Life education workshop at the Second Life community convention (pp. 13-18). CA, San Francisco: The University Of Paisley.

Kennedy, D., Vozdolska, R., & McComb, S. (2010). Team decision making in computer-supported cooperative work: How initial computer-mediated or face-to-face meetings set the stage for later outcomes. *Decision Sciences, 41*(4), 933–954.

Khan, B. (2005). *Managing e-learning strategies: Design, delivery, implementation and evaluation.* Hershey, PA: Information Science Publishing.

Kidd, T. T., & Chen, I. (2009). *Wired for Learning: An Educator's Guide to Web 2.0.* Iap.

Kilpatrick, S., Field, J., & Falk, I. (2003). Social capital: An analytical tool for exploring lifelong learning and community development investigator. *British Educational Research Journal, 29*(3), 417-433.

Kim, D., & Lee, R. P. (2010). Systems Collaboration and Strategic Collaboration: Their Impacts on Supply Chain Responsiveness and Market Performance. *Decision Sciences*, *41*(4), 955-981.

Kimball, L. (1997). Managing virtual teams. In *Text of speech given at Team Strategies Conference sponsored by Federated Press, Toronto, Canada.*

Kini, A., & Choobineh, J. (1998). Trust in electronic commerce: Definition and theoretical considerations. *31st Annual Hawaii International Conference on System Sciences, 4,* 51–61.

Kirkman, B., & Mathieu, J. (2005). The dimensions and antecedents of team virtuality. *Journal of Management, 31*, 700–718.

Kirkman, B., Rosen, B., Gibson, C., Tesluk, P., & McPherson, S. (2002). Five challenges to virtual team success: Lessons from Sabre, Inc. *Academy of Management Executive, 16*(3), 67–79.

Konradt, U., Filip, R., & Hoffmann, S. (2003). Flow experience and positive affect during hypermedia learning. *British Journal of Educational Technology, 34*, 309–327.

Konstantinidis, A., Tsiatsos, T., & Pomportsis, A. (2009). Collaborative virtual learning environments: Design and evaluation. *Multimedia Tools and Applications, 44*, 279–304. Retrieved from ABI/INFORM Global. (Document ID: 1894423431)

Kramer, R. M., & Brewer, M. B. (1986). Social group identity and the emergence of cooperation in resource conservation dilemmas. In Wilke, C., Rutte, D., & Messick, M. (Eds.), *Experimental studies of social dilemmas* (pp. 205–234). Frankfurt: Peter Lang.

Krebs, S. A., Hobman, E. V., & Bordia, P. (2006). Virtual teams and group member dissimilarity: Consequences for the development of trust. *Small Group Research, 37*, 721–741.

Kristeva, Julia. "Word, Dialogue, and Novel." *Desire and Language*. Ed. Leon S. Roudiez. Trans. Thomas Gora et al. New York: Columbia UP, 1980. 64-91.

Kvale, D. (1996). *Interviews.* London: SAGE Publications.

KZERO. (2008). *Virtual worlds markets: Key strategies deployed in 2008 and predictions for 2009*. Los Angeles: K Zero Consultancy. Retrieved from www.kzero.co.uk/blog/category/conferences

Lacy. S. (2012). Philip Rosedale: The media is wrong, SecondLife didn't fail. *PandoDaily*. Retrieved from http://pandodaily.com/2012/07/06/philip-rosedale-the-media-is-wrong-secondlife-didnt-fail/

Langfred, C. W. (1998). Is group cohesiveness a double-edged sword? An investigation of the effects of cohesiveness on performance. *Small Group Research, 29*, 124-143.

Lancey, D. (1993). *Qualitative research in education: An introduction to the major traditions*. New York: Longman.

Lauritzen, C., & Jaegar, M. (1997). *Integrating learning through story: The narrative curriculum.* Albany, NY: Delmar Publishers.

Lawrie, A. (1999). *The new Fontana dictionary of modern thought.* HarperCollins.

Lawrence-Lightfoot, S., & Hoffman Davis, J. (1997). *The art and science of portraiture*. San Francisco, CA: Jossey Bass.

Lawrie, A. (1999). *The new Fontana dictionary of modern thought.* HarperCollins.

Linden Lab. (2006, October 25). Second Life security bulletin. *Internet Archive*. Retrieved from http://web.archive.org/web/20061025064746/http:/secondlife.com/corporate/bulletin.php

Linden Lab. (2012). Linden Lab official: Technical overview of Second Life security. Retrieved from http://wiki.secondlife.com/wiki/Linden_Lab_Official:Technical_overview_of_Second_Life_security

Linden Research Inc. (n.d.). Linden Lab, where worlds are born. Retrieved from http://lindenlab.com.

Linden Research Inc. (2011). *Second Life education: The virtual learning advantage*. Retrieved from http://lecs-static-secondlife-com.s3.amazonaws.com/work/SL-Edu-Brochure-010411.pdf

Lindlof, T. (1995). *Qualitative communication research methods*. Thousand Oaks, CA: Sage.

Lipnack, J., & Stamps, J. (1997). *Virtual teams: Reaching across space, time, and organizations with technology*. New York: John Wiley & Sons, Inc.

Livingstone, D., Kemp, J., and Edgar, E. (2008). From multi-user virtual environment to 3-D virtual learning environment. *Research in Learning Technology 16*(3), 139–150.

Levy, S. (2008). Steven Levy on melding the digital and physical realms. *Wired Magazine, 16*(11). Retrieved from http://www.wired.com/gadgets/gadgetreviews/magazine/16-11/ts_levy

Lu, T., Chiang, C., Lin, M., & Lee, C. (1998). A collaborative scene editor for VRML worlds. *Computer Graphics Forum, 17*(3), 53–61.

Malaby, T. M. (2009). *Making virtual worlds: Linden Lab and Second Life*. Ithaca, N.Y.: Cornell University Press.

Mancuso, D. S., Chluo, D. T., & McWhorter, R. (2010). A study of adult learning in a virtual world. *Advances in Developing Human Resources, 12*, 681–699. doi:10.1177/1523422410395368

Marinaccio, M. J. (2007). *Organization Structure and Its Impact on the Power/politic Dynamic: A Mixed Method Exploration of Senior Management Perceptions of Formal and Virtual Organizations*. ProQuest.

Marks, M., Mathieu, J., & Zaccaro, S. (2001). A temporally based framework and taxonomy of team processes. *Academy of Management Review, 26*, 356–376.

Martins, L., Gilson, L., & Maynard, M. (2004). Virtual teams: What do we know and where do we go from here? *Journal of Management, 30*, 805–835. doi:10.1016/j.jm.2004.05.002

Mathieu, J., Gilson, L., & Ruddy, T. (2006). Empowerment and team effectiveness: An empirical test of an integrated model. *Journal of Applied Psychology, 91*(1), 97–108. doi:10.1037/0021-9010.91.1.97

Mathieu, J. E., DeShon, R. P., & Bergh, D. (2008). Meditational inferences in organizational research: Then, now, and beyond. *Organizational Research Methods, 11*, 203–223.

Maxim, B. R. (2008). Campus of hope: Using the virtual world to improve our world. Retrieved from http://slurl.com/secondlife/UM%20Dearborn/236/26/21

Maxim, B. R., Sable, M. D., & Cristiano, J. (2010, October). Service learning and virtual worlds. In *Frontiers in Education Conference (FIE), 2010 IEEE* (pp. T2D-1). IEEE. doi: 10.1109/FIE.2010.5673328

Maxwell, J. A. (2005). *Qualitative research design: An interactive approach* (2nd ed.). Thousand Oaks, CA: Sage.

Maxwell, J. A. (2008). *Applied research designs: Designing a qualitative study (chapter 7)*. Retrieved from http://www.engin.umich.edu/teaching/crltengin/engineering-education-research-resouces/maxwell-designing-a-qualitative-study.pdf

Mayer, R. C., Davis, J. H., & Schoorman, F. D. (1995). An integrative model of organizational trust. *Academy of Management Review, 20*(3), 709-734.

Maznevski, M., & Chudoba, K. (2000). Bridging space over time: Global virtual team dynamics and effectiveness. *Organization Science, 11*, 473–492.

Mennecke, B. E., McNeill, D., Ganis, M., Roche, E. M., Bray, D. A., Konsynski, B., . . . & Lester, J. (2008). Second Life and other virtual worlds: A roadmap for research. *Communications of the Association for Information Systems*, *22*(20), 371-388.

Messinger, P. R., Stroulia, E., Lyons, K., Bone, M., Niu, R. H., Smirnov, K., & Perelgut, S. (2009). Virtual worlds—past, present, and future: New directions in social computing. *Decision Support Systems, 47*(3), 204-228. doi:10.1016/j.dss.2009.02.014

Metcalf, S., & Dede, C. (2011). *Dive into virtual worlds: Learning about ecosystems through immersion.* Retrieved from http://www.isteconference.org/conferences/ISTE/2011/handout_uploads/KEY_60766537/Metcalf_ISTE2011 EcoMUVEtalk.pdf

Meyerson, D., Weick, K. E., & Kramer, R. M. (1996). Swift trust and temporary groups. In M. Kramer & T. R. Tyler (Eds.), *Trust in organizations: Frontiers of theory and research* (pp. 166–195). Thousand Oaks, CA: Sage.

Nelson, K. (1989). *Narratives from the crib.* Cambridge, MA: Harvard University Press.

Nesson, R., & Nesson, C. (2008). The case for education in virtual worlds. *Space and Culture, 11*, 273–284. doi:10.1177/1206331208319149

New Media Consortium (2009). *Developing new learning and collaboration environments for education.* Retrieved from http://www.vreflections.com/Second%20Life/NMC.htm

New Media Consortium (2012). NMC virtual worlds. Retrieved from: http://www.nmc.org/projects/virtual-worlds

Noble, S. (2002). *Starting up a virtual team.* Retrieved from http://www.teambuildinginc.com/article_virtual.htm

O'Hara-Devereaux, M., & Johansen, R. (1994). *Global work: Bridging distance, culture, and time.* San Francisco, CA: Jossey-Bass.

Ondrejka, C. (2008). Education unleashed: Participatory culture, education, and innovation in Second Life. In K. Salen (Ed.), *The ecology of games: Connecting youth, games, and learning* (pp. 229–251). Cambridge, MA: MIT Press.

Owens, D., Mitchell, A., Khazanchi, D. and Ilze Zigurs (2011, February). An empirical investigation of virtual world projects and metaverse technology capabilities. *SIGMIS Data Base for Advances in Information Systems*, 42(1), 74-101.

Patton, M. Q. (2000). *Qualitative research and evaluation methods.* London: SAGE Publications.

Peters, L. M., and Manz, C. C. (2007). Identifying antecedents of virtual team collaboration. *Team Performance Management, 13*(3/4), 117-129.

Petrakou, A. (2010). Interacting through avatars: Virtual worlds as a context for online education. *Computers & Education, 54*, 1020–1027.

Powell, A., Piccoli, G., & Ives, B. (2004). Virtual teams: A review of current literature and directions for future research. *Data Base for Advances in Information Systems, 35*(1), 6–36.

Priest, S. H. (2008). North American audiences for news of emerging technologies: Canadian and US responses to bio- and nanotechnologies. *Journal of Risk Research, 11*, 877–889. doi:10.1080/1366987080205690

Putnam, R. D. (1995). Bowling alone: America's declining social capital. *Journal of Democracy, 6*, 65–78.

Ratcheva, V., & Vyakarnam, S. (2001). Exploring team formation processes in virtual partnerships. *Integrated Manufacturing Systems*, *12*(7), 512-524.

Reave, L. (2005). Spiritual values and practices related to leadership effectiveness. *Leadership Quarterly, 16*, 655–687.

Ricoeur, P. (1991). Explanation and understanding. In K. Blamey and J. Thompson (Eds), *From text to action.* Evanston, IL: Northwestern University Press.

Ricoeur, P. (1988). Humans as the subject matter of philosophy. In T. P. Kemp and D. Rasmussen (Eds.), *The narrative path: The later works of Paul Ricoeur*. Cambridge, MA: MIT Press.

Reeves, B., & Read, J. L. (2009). *Total engagement: using games and virtual worlds to change the way people work and businesses compete*. Boston: Harvard Business Press.

Reina, D., & Reina, M. (2006). *Trust and betrayal in the workplace: Building effective relationships in your organization.* San Francisco: Berrett - Koehler.

Richardson, L. (2000). Writing: A method of inquiry. In N.K. Denzon & Y.S. Lincoln (Eds.), *Handbook of qualitative research* (2nd ed., pp. 923-948). Thousand Oaks, CA: Sage.

Riedl, M. O., Stern, A., Dini, D., & Alderman, J. (2008). Dynamic experience management in virtual worlds for entertainment, education, and training.*International Transactions on Systems Science and Applications, Special Issue on Agent Based Systems for Human Learning*, *4*(2), 23-42.

Riessman, C. K. (1993). *Narrative analysis* (Vol. 30). Newbury Park, CA: Sage Publications.

Riffaterre, M. (1994). Intertextuality vs. hypertextuality. *New Literary History*,*25*(4), 779-788.

Riggs, B., & Shimmin, B. (2008). *Virtual worlds not quite virtually there for business communications and collaboration.* Advisory Report: Enterprise Technology and Software. Washington DC. Retrieved from http://www.marketresearch.com/Current-Analysis-Inc-v2495/Virtual-Worlds-Quite-Virtually-Business-2047428/

Rindova, V. P., Petkova, A. P., & Kotha, S. (2007). Standing out: How new firms in emerging markets build reputation. *Strategic Organization, 5*, 31–70. doi:10.1177/1476127006074389

Ripamonti, F. (2009). Language teachers in virtual worlds: Or how to create a digital euphoria with Web 2.0 tools, interactive boards and mash ups. *Proceedings of the International Conference "ICT for Language Learning"* (3rd ed.). Retrieved from http://www.pixel-online.net/ICT4LL2010/common/download/Proceedings_pdf/IBL46-Ripamonti.pdf

Robbins, S. (2007). A futurist's view of Second Life education: A developing taxonomy of digital spaces. In D. Livingstone & J. Kemp (Eds.), *Proceedings of the Second Life Education Workshop Community Convention* (pp. 27–33). Chicago, IL: University of Paisley.

Robison, L., Schmid, A., & Siles, M. (2002). Is social capital really capital? *Review of Social Economy, 60*, 1–24.

Roger, T., & Johnson, D. W. (1994). An overview of cooperative learning. In J. Thousand, A. Villa, and A. Nevin (Eds.), *Creativity and collaborative learning.* 87-101. Baltimore: Brookes Press.

Rubin, H. J., & Rubin, S. (2005). *Qualitative interviewing: The art of hearing data.* Thousand Oaks, CA: Sage.

Ryan, G. W., & Bernard, H. R. (2000). Data management and analysis methods. In N. K. Denzin & Y. S. Lincoln (Eds.), *Handbook of qualitative research* (2nd ed., pp. 769–802). Thousand Oaks, CA: Sage.

Sarker, S., Sarker, S., Chatterjee, S., & Valacich, J. S. (2010). Media effects on group collaboration: An empirical examination in an ethical decision-making context. *Decision Sciences, 41*(4), 887-931.

Schultze, U., & Orlikowski, W. J. (2010). Virtual worlds: A performative perspective on globally distributed, immersive work. *Information Systems Research, 21*, 810–821. doi:10.1287/isre.1100.0321

Seiler, J. (2009). 76% of enterprise executives predict rise in virtual events for 2009. Retrieved from http://www.engagedigital.com/blog/2009/01/30/76-of-enterprise-executives-predict-rise-in-virtual-events-for-2009-3/

Serrat, O. (2009, August). *Managing virtual teams*. Retrieved from http://www.adb.org/sites/default/files/pub/2009/managing-virtual-teams.pdf

Shernoff, D., Csikszentmihalyi, M., Schneider, B., & Shernoff, E. S. (2003). Student engagement in high school classrooms from the perspective of flow theory. *School Psychology Quarterly, 18*, 158–176.

Shepard, T. (2013). Second Life grid survey — economic metrics. Retrieved from http://www.gridsurvey.com/economy.php

Silver, C., & Fielding, N. (2008). Using computer packages in qualitative research. *The SAGE handbook of qualitative research in psychology*, 334-369.

Skadberg, Y. X., & Kimmel, J. R. (2004). Visitors' flow experience while browsing a web site: Its measurement, contributing factors and consequences. *Computers in Human Behavior, 20*, 403–422.

Slife, B. D., & Williams, R. (1995). *What's behind the research? Discovering hidden assumptions in the behavioral sciences*. Thousand Oaks, CA: Sage.

SLOODLE. (2011). *SLOODLE: Simulation linked object oriented dynamic learning environment project page*. Retrieved from http://www.sloodle.org/

Strauss, A. & Corbin, J. (1990). *Basics of qualitative research: Grounded theory procedures and techniques*. Newberry Park, CA: SAGE Publications.

Suchan, J., & Hayzak, G. (2001). The communication characteristics of virtual teams: A case study. *IEEE Transactions on Professional Communication*, 44, 174–186.

Sundstrom, E., DeMuse, K. P. and Futrell, D. (1990). Work teams: Applications and effectiveness. *American Psychologist, 45,* 120-133.

Takahashi, D. (2010). Founder replaces CEO of Second Life maker Linden Lab. Retrieved from http://venturebeat.com/2010/06/24/linden-lab-ceo-resigns-founder-returns-as-interim-boss/

Thompson, C. (2011). Next-generation virtual worlds: Architecture, status, and directions. *IEEE Internet Computing, 15*, 60–65. Retrieved from ProQuest Computing. (Document ID: 2220194991)

Thompson, L., & Nadler, J. (2002). Negotiating via information technology: Theory and application. *Journal of Social Issues, (58)*1, 109-124.

Trochim, W. M. K. (2002). *The research methods knowledge base* (2nd ed.). Retrieved from http://www.socialresearchmethods.net/kb (version current as of October 20, 2006).

Tuten, T. (2009). Real world experience, virtual world environment: The design and execution of marketing plans in Second Life. *Marketing Education Review, 19*(1), 1–5.

Ubell, R. (2010). Virtual TEAM learning. *T+D, 64*(8), 52–57.

Uribe Larach, D., & Cabra, J. (2010). Creative problem solving in Second Life: An action research study. *Creativity & Innovation Management, 19*, 167–179. doi:10.1111/j.1467-8691.2010.00550.x

Walther, J. B. (1995). Relational aspects of computer-mediated communication: Experimental observations over time. *Organization Science, 6*, 186–203.

Walther, J. B. (1996). Computer-mediated communication: Impersonal, interpersonal, and hyperpersonal interaction. *Communication Research, 23*, 3–43.

Walther, J. (1997). Group and interpersonal effects in international computer-mediated collaboration. *Human Communication Research, 23*, 342–369. doi:10.1111/j.1468-2958.1997.tb00400

Walther, J. B., & Burgoon, J. K. (1992). Relational communication in computer-mediated interaction. *Human Communication Research, 19*(1), 50–88.

Ward, D. (2009). Editorial review. *Library Journal, 134*(9), 89. Retrieved from http://books.google.com/books?id=0PWpblV3bWMC&dq=what+caused+the+rise+of+virtual+worlds&lr=&source=gbs_navlinks_s

Warkentin, M., & Beranek, P. (1999). Training to improve virtual team communication. *Information Systems Journal, 9*, 271–289. doi:10.1046/j.1365-2575.1999.00065.x

Wasko, M., Teigland, R., Leidner, D., & Jarvenpaa, S. (2011). Stepping into the internet: New ventures in virtual worlds. *MIS Quarterly, 35*, 645–652. doi:10.1111/j.1468-2958.1997.tb00400

Wenger, E. (1998). *Communities of practice: learning, meaning, and identity*. New York: Cambridge University Press.

Wenger, E. (2001). Supporting communities of practice. A survey of community-oriented technologies.

Wenger, E., McDermott, R., & Snyder, W. M. (2002). *Cultivating communities of practice: A guide to managing knowledge*. Boston.: Harvard Business School Press.

Wenner, L. A. (2010). Mocking the fan for fun and profit: Sports dirt, fanship identity, and commercial narratives. In A.C. Billings (Ed.), *Sports media: Transformation, integration, consumption*. London and New York: Routledge (in press).

Wiecha, J., Heyden, R., Sternthal, E., & Merialdi, M. (2010). Learning in a virtual world: Experience with using Second Life for medical education. *Journal of Medical Internet Research, 12*(1), e1. Retrieved from http://www.jmir.org/2010/1/e1/

Williams, D. (2010). The mapping principle and a research framework for virtual worlds. *Communication Theory, 20*, 451–470. Retrieved from Research Library. (Document ID: 2169036631)

Wyld, D. C. (2008). *Government in 3-D: How public leaders can draw on virtual worlds*. Retrieved from http://www.businessofgovernment.org/publications/grant_reports/details/index.asp?gid=332

Yolles, M. (2007). The dynamics of narrative and antenarrative and their relation to story. *Journal of Organizational Change Management, 20*(1), 74–94.

Yu, X., Owens, D., & Khazanchi, D. (2012). Building socioemotional environments in metaverses for virtual teams in healthcare: A conceptual exploration. *Health Information Science*, Berlin: Springer, 4-12.

Zaccaro, S. J., Rittman, A. L., & Marks, M. A. (2001). Team leadership. *Leadership Quarterly, 12*, 451–483.

Zolin, R., Hinds, P. J., Fruchter, R., and Levitt, R. E. (2004). Interpersonal trust in cross-functional, geographically distributed work: A longitudinal study. *Information and Organization,* 14, 1-26.

Zornoza, A., Orengo, V., & Peñarroja, V. (2009). Relational capital in virtual teams: The role played by trust. *Social Science Information, 48*, 257–281. doi:10.1177/0539018409102414

Appendices

APPENDIX A: INFORMED CONSENT

Informed Consent Notecard

Title of Study: Building Collaborative Learning Environments: The Effects of Trust and Its Relationship to Learning in the 3-D Virtual Education Environment of Second Life

Investigator: Christina B. Steele (Xavia Zuta in Second Life)

Contact Number: (801)643-8090

Purpose of the Study

You are invited to participate in a research study. This study is under the direction of Dr. Anne-Marie Armstrong, faculty at the Institute of Advanced Studies, CTU where the investigator am a Doctorate of Computer Science (DCS) student. The purpose of this research study is to examine the stories of educators who have had an experience with building trust in the virtual classroom. The purpose of this qualitative study is to describe how emerging media are utilized to facilitate trust as a component of social capital in virtual environments. The goal is to identify the behaviors that create trust and to develop recommendations to assist learning and explore what educators can do to help students learn in a virtual classroom. This study seeks to address the published research deficiencies and will contribute a qualitative analysis that will address the deficiencies by helping to further understand the perception of the role of trust in virtual classrooms. This analysis will build a rich, detailed description of the role of trust in the virtual world environment for educators. The study will identify similarities and differences in studies focusing on virtual worlds. From the study, the research explores the concept of a learning environment and how social capital can cause the educator to succeed or fail in the purpose of facilitating the learning experience in virtual worlds. To this end, the investigator will seek to combine themes from educator stories that describe these factors. The investigator was presenting the results of my research in Second Life at the end of July 2013. You are more than welcome to attend this event, and the investigator will make sure to get you the details and an invitation.

Participants

You are being asked to participate in the study if you have used Second Life as an Educator. You was asked to describe your experiences. This is not a clinical or diagnostic interview. You may refuse to answer any questions, without explanation.

Procedures

If you volunteer to participate in this study, you was asked to do the following: The investigator was employing a Qualitative Research Design using Narrative Methods. Specifically, storytelling was used as the approach to explore the issue of trust in virtual educational environments for educators. To study this, stories was collected of experiences with teaching in the virtual world of Second Life using a narrative approach. Educators was interviewed at some length to determine how they have personally experienced trust in this context.

You can find out more about this research project at my blog http://www.christinasteele.blogspot.com/ or, Instant Message (IM) me anytime in Second Life.

For further information, or to verify this project is legitimate, you may contact my faculty advisor, Dr. Anne-Marie Armstrong at aarmstrong@coloradotech.edu.

Benefits of Participation

There may/may not be direct benefits to you as a participant in this study. However, this study hopes to provide a foundation for educators to be able to identify ways in which a collaborative learning environment can be established through trust. As Dickey (2005) cited, benefits include being able to experiment without concern for real-world repercussions and being able to learn by doing, whereas Ondrejka (as cited in Eschenbrenner et al., 2008) mentioned a greater level of comfort in asking questions and an ability to develop a sense of shared learning, while Conway (as cited in Eschenbrenner et al., 2008) cited that the virtual environment could provide opportunities to introduce more creativity into the classroom.

Risks of Participation

There are risks involved in all research studies. This study is estimated to involve minimal risk. An example of this risk is possibly feeling uncomfortable answering questions about your experiences. Although no study is completely risk-free, no harm or distress risks from participation have been identified at this time. If at any time you become uncomfortable, you may cease participation at any time. The results of the research study was published, but the name or identity of the participants will not be revealed. All information collected was confidential.

Cost/Compensation

This was no financial cost to you to participate in this study. The study will take approximately 45 – 60 minutes to complete. You will not be compensated for your time. *Colorado Technical University will not provide compensation or free medical care for an unanticipated injury sustained as a result of participating in this research study.*

Contact Information

If you have any questions or concerns about the study, you may contact the investigator, Christina B. Steele, c.steele15@my.cs.coloradotech.edu or at (801)643-8090 or via IM to my avatar in Second Life (Xavia Zuta). You may also contact my doctoral committee chair Dr. Anne-Marie Armstrong at aarmstrong@coloradotech.edu, or at 734-301-3011. For questions regarding the rights of research subjects, any complaints or comments regarding the manner in which the study is being conducted, you may contact Colorado Technical University – Doctoral Programs at 719-598-0200.

Voluntary Participation

Your participation in this study is completely voluntary. You may refuse to participate in this study or in any part of this study. You may withdraw at any time without prejudice to your relations with the university. You are encouraged to ask questions about this study at the beginning or at any time during the research study.

Confidentiality

All information gathered in this study was kept completely confidential. No reference was made in written or oral materials that could link you to this study. According to Linden Labs (2012), the Second Life client login uses password-only authentication over secure HTTP. At no time does Linden Lab have access the passwords itself. Password and any information entered through the "My Account" page on the Second Life website is encrypted and uses a secure HTTP connection.

Additionally, the Second Life Viewer provides a connection to Second Life, which does not compromise the computer's security. At this time, there is no known remote exploit to the client. The viewer also uses a Vivox-plugin for spatial and group voice chat, which is quality checked and provided exclusively by Linden Lab. The viewer does not use any other third-party plugins, nor is there currently a plugin architecture. Private Regions can be set-up as part of an Estate in the Second Life world. These Regions provide a highly manageable environment for conducting private business in the virtual world of Second Life, ensuring that only approved users can enter the Region. A Private Region is secure from eavesdropping. The Region is surrounded by an equivalent void space, represented by water; void space cannot be crossed by walking, running, flying, or by camera.

There currently is no Linden Scripting Language (LSL) script which can listen to Instant Messages, voice communication, or media streams, nor can an LSL script directly capture visual content such as objects or textures.

This informed consent form was given to your avatar via a notecard. Notecards are the simple text documents that you can create and share in Second Life. Please sign this form by typing your real life name below, saving and submitting back to the researcher (Xavia Zuta). Second Life secures notecards from unauthorized access, use or disclosure. Therefore, personally identifiable information which you may provide on the computer was stored on servers in a controlled, secure environment, protected from unauthorized access, use or disclosure. If personal information (such as a name, age, etc…) is transmitted, it is protected through the use of encryption, such as the Secure Socket Layer (SSL) protocol. The notecards was securely stored on the investigator's external hard drive. This drive will then be secured in a safe until the 3-year expiration is due at which time the data was securely wiped.

Participant Consent

I have read the above information and agree to participate in this study. I am at least 18 years of age. A copy of this form has been given to me. By typing my name below and returning this notecard to the investigator, I accept the terms of this informed consent form.

______________________________________ ______________________

Signature of Participant Date

APPENDIX B: DETAILED SOLICITATION

Seeking participants for VW research on trust and learning in SL (Christina Steele) *Title of Study*: Building Collaborative Learning Environments: The Effects of Trust and Its Relationship to Learning in the 3-D Virtual Education Environment of Second Life

Investigator: Christina B. Steele (Xavia Zuta in Second Life)

Purpose of the Study

You are invited to participate in a research study. This study is under the direction of Dr. Anne-Marie Armstrong, faculty at Institute of Advanced Studies, CTU where the investigator am a Doctorate of Computer Science (DCS) student. The purpose of this research study is to examine the stories of educators who have had an experience with building trust in the virtual classroom. The purpose of this qualitative study is to describe how emerging media are utilized to facilitate trust as a component of social capital in virtual environments. The goal is to identify the behaviors that create trust and to develop recommendations to assist learning and explore what educators can do to help students learn in a virtual classroom. This study seeks to address the published research deficiencies and will contribute a qualitative analysis that will address the deficiencies by helping to further understand the perception of the role of trust in virtual classrooms. This analysis will build a rich, detailed description of the role of trust in the virtual world environment for educators. The study will identify similarities and differences in studies focusing on virtual worlds. From the study, the research explores the concept of a learning environment and how social capital can cause the educator to succeed or fail in the purpose of facilitating the learning experience in virtual worlds. To this end, the investigator will seek to combine themes from educator stories that describe these factors. The investigator was presenting the results of my research in Second Life at the end of July 2013. You are more than welcome to attend this event, and the investigator will make sure to get you the details and an invitation.

Participants

You are being asked to participate in the study if you have used Second Life as an Educator. You was asked to describe your experiences. This is not a clinical or diagnostic interview. You may refuse to answer any questions, without explanation. If you are interested please sign up via the following survey link: http://www.surveymonkey.com/s/58G6K6C You can find out more about this research project at my blog http://www.christinasteele.blogspot.com/ or, Instant Message (IM) me anytime in Second Life. Christina B. Steele (aka Xavia Zuta)
Doctoral Candidate
Institute of Advanced Studies
Colorado Technical University

APPENDIX C: DISSERTATION RESEARCH LOG

Respondent Data

#	Started	Time	Code	City/Town	State Province	Country:	SL Ed Exp & 18+	Informed Consent	School	Grade Level	Time In SL
1	Friday, October 05, 2012 12:12:45 AM	3 mins		Syros		Greece	Yes	Accept			
2	Friday, October 05, 2012 1:55:06 PM	2 mins	P5	Greenville		USA	Yes	Accept	East Carolina University	Higher Ed	5yrs 9 mths
3	Tuesday, November 13, 2012 1:08:49 PM	14 mins		Kildare Town		Ireland	Yes	Accept			4yrs
4	Tuesday, November 13, 2012 1:31:17 PM	2 mins		Highland		USA	Yes	Accept	Indiana University Northwest	Higher Ed	5yrs
5	Tuesday, November 13, 2012 2:27:49 PM	3 mins		Chicago		USA	Yes	Accept	DePaul University	Higher Ed	Syros
6	Tuesday, November 13, 2012 2:52:41 PM	1 min		Cheyney	Cyclades	USA	Yes	Accept	Cheyney University	Higher Ed	
7	Tuesday, November 13, 2012 5:02:32 PM	4 mins		Paris		France	Yes	Accept			
8	Wednesday, November 14, 2012 3:28:22 AM	3 mins	S6	Curitiba		Brasil	Yes	Accept	Federal University of Parana	Higher Ed	6yrs
9	Wednesday, November 14, 2012 8:19:36 AM	3 mins		Lumby		Canada	Yes	Accept	U of Calgary	Higher Ed	
10	Thursday, November 15, 2012 12:19:50 PM	2 mins		Gary	Illinois	USA	Yes	Accept	Indiana University Northwest	Higher Ed	1yr
11	Monday, November 19, 2012 7:58:56 AM	3 mins		Bristol	PA	USA	Yes	Accept		Higher Ed	4yrs
12	Friday, December 07, 2012 9:45:36 AM	1 min		University Park	Parana	UK	Yes	Accept	U of the West of England	Higher Ed	4yrs
13	Tuesday, January 15, 2013 9:48:14 AM	11 mins	S5		Pennsylvania	USA	Yes	Accept	Penn State University	Higher Ed	6yrs
14	Tuesday, January 15, 2013 10:46:04 AM	25 mins			Co. Kildare	Ireland	Yes	Accept	Computer Education Society		6yrs
15	Tuesday, January 15, 2013 2:34:39 PM	37 mins	P4		PA	USA	Yes	Accept			5 yrs
16	Tuesday, January 15, 2013 5:16:54 PM	1 min				Fiji	Yes	Accept			5 yrs
17	Wednesday, January 16, 2013 2:10:41 AM	4 mins				Greece	Yes	Accept			
18	Wednesday, January 16, 2013 9:03:00 AM	57 mins	S4 P3			USA	Yes	Accept	Alternative Youth Activities	9th-12th	4 yrs
19	Wednesday, January 16, 2013 9:43:59 AM	40 mins	P2	Oxford		UK	Yes	Accept	RM Education	ALL	6yrs
20	Thursday, January 17, 2013 5:15:05 AM	2 mins		Bristol	Cyclades	UK	Yes	Accept	U of the West of England	Higher Ed	
21	Thursday, January 17, 2013 7:11:35 AM	7 mins	S3 P1	Greenville	Oregon	USA	Yes	Accept	East Carolina University	ALL	7 years
22	Friday, January 18, 2013 10:41:31 AM	4 mins		Syros		Greece	Yes	Accept	U of the Aegean	Higher Ed	
23	Monday, February 04, 2013 2:48:33 PM	3 mins	S2	Orlando	NC	USA	Yes	Accept	US Navy	Higher Ed	6 yrs
24	Monday, February 18, 2013 10:29:01 AM	33 mins	S1	Roseburg	Cyclades	USA	Yes	Accept	Phoenix Charter School	Pre-K - 12th	
SL 1	1/20/13 8:27	20 mins	P6			Tawian	Yes	Accept	Visiting Associate Professor, Tainan Arts University, Taiwan	Higher Ed	5yrs 10 mths
SL 2	11/16/12 8:42AM	32 mins	P7			Greece	Yes	Accept	University of the Aegean	Higher Ed	7 years

Survey Data – left numbers & top letters used for analysis references

	A	B	C	D	E
1	**What is your experience with building trust in virtual teams (teams of students, teams of educators, or virtual education environments)?**	**How did you know that trust had been built?**	**What was the effect of building trust in a virtual world on the learning?**	**How would you describe building trust in a virtual environment?**	**What are your perceptions of how your development of trust evolved?**
2	I have worked with teaching and professional teams in providing education in college access programs, as well as with teams of educators and facilitators in other social groups (relationship-oriented sims and roleplay sims).	We were able to communicate effectively and team members felt able to present concerns, ideas, suggestions for improvement, as well as to handle misunderstandings within the group. The groups have continued to work together - the longest group working together for over 4 years.	Being better able to meet the needs of learners; being able to expand educational opportunities, to be able to be used as a model for other administration units (like sim management).	It's a long-term process which can be difficult, given the lack of face time and ability to read body language and facial expression. Adding voice to meetings or augmenting it with Skype was helpful in improving clarity of communication. Time zones can be a challenge to finding mutually agreeable meeting times as well.	Time and patience is really required. Over time, those who were really committed to the process and the team emerged by their willingness to continue to be active in the team and weather changes in the team and sim organization and management. Leaders emerge over time and as they learned that the team was a safe place to be able to express their abilities and talents, they would step forward to initiate new projects.
3	I have been using virtual environments as a learning area both in the classroom and at a distance for 3 years in a high school setting. I have had limited success with building trust in the virtual world but have been able to physically meet with my students and then build an in-world relationship.	Perhaps I need a definition of the way trust is being used, if it is a typical teacher student relationship of educational guidance and trust, I would have to say when students feel comfortable to make mistakes and share them with me.	Perhaps the ability to laugh and play around yet help students to refocus when necessary. My goal is always to foster a collaborative environment that fosters creativity in my students.	The ability of students to act naturally (yet with respect) and to push their personal limits because of a trusting guide who will support when possible and redirect when necessary.	As my curriculum became more project based and I allowed the students more freedom to choose I lost "typical" teacher control of my class. As students succeed more and took on more challenging projects I trust them more and perhaps in return they trusted me

					more.
4	My experience involves working with faculty members to create group simulations in which students work together to accomplish a task or critical thinking skill.	The faculty requires students to keep journals, talk through chat about their experience, or to write a paper on their experience in working with others, how the experience helped their learning, and how they used it to accomplish the course goals.	The students reported getting a lot out of the simulations but also reported some group activities were not as successful as they could have been because not all group members participated equally.	Trust is working with others successfully in a virtual environment, getting to know the person behind the avatar through chat or voice. There is a certain trust that is developed when talking to another avatar and becoming familiar with them.	Trust evolves as it does in real life by working with other avatars regularly through a class. Trust can also be developed when meeting other people in SL and extending the learning beyond the classroom.
5	It takes time. And it takes interaction. My course is an 8 week course and I feel like trust begins to develop by the end.	Commitments are made, and follow-up happens. People are prompt and attentive - more dynamically active.	Learning increases.		
6	I have been incorporating Second Life Virtual worlds in my technology education program for the past 3 years. Students are usually willing to jump in and get to work. Educators on the other hand are very resistant to bringing Second Life into their curriculum. In three years I have had 2 teachers that have been willing to make that step.	Watching students work together and talk through large scale projects together, develop a direction, assign tasks and responsibilities, and work together to see the project to completion. I know trust has been built when educators freely share their lesson plans, projects, outcomes, the educational process (both good and not so good), and share ideas including cooperative learning experiences.	Personally I believe that trust is the one key factor to building a valid educational community in the virtual world. Without trust the virtual experience is limited only to the classroom. For example, I am trying to rewrite the Global Studies curriculum. Move Global Studies into the virtual world where students and educators can work together building a neutral place where students compare, contrast, share, discuss, and exchange ideas and thoughts about where they live, what is happening at that moment in time in their lives. Imagine what the class could look like! Students talking about the geography of where they live in Japan, South Africa, France, or Germany. Then moving that same discussion to the political aspects of each country. Students making and uploading videos to document and share their portion of a project then compiling all the smaller projects into a group project where each student, country, culture, and point of view are shared and discussed. As it is projects and ideas such as this one are stalled because educators and administrators are letting fear and mistrust keep them from even giving it a serious look.	As with anything, I believe leading by example is the only plausible first step. In other words, when I first meet someone and want to share my virtual educational experience, once I know for certain that they are who they say they are. I give them a look at our Second Life Island. I show them how and why we do what we do. I make all of my resources, curriculum, projects, and materials are available to them at no cost. I will allow them to bring their students on our island and work with our students.	This is easy for me. I was the first. I did everything on my own. The only person to trust was me.

Interview Data - left numbers & top letters used for analysis references

			F	G
	Started	Mins	Txt Log	Interview Notes
7	1/24/13 12:40PM	26	[2013/01/24 12:44] XZ: great! so to start, can you tell me , What is your experience with building trust in virtual teams? [2013/01/24 12:45] P1: I have several programs where we build trust with virtual teams by working with different school systems [2013/01/24 12:45] P1: they are high school system with students and facilitators [2013/01/24 12:46] XZ: Great, so how would you describe the effect of building trust in a virtual world on the learning environment? [2013/01/24 12:47] P1: I think if done correctly, it resembles the trust you can initiate in a face-to-face encounter [2013/01/24 12:47] P1: and that students can interact effectively with faculty and vice-versa to create a cohesive learning environment [2013/01/24 12:48] P1: it is also my experience that students seem to speak up more through chat or voice in an online virtual environment, they seem to feel a bit protected through the avatar [2013/01/24 12:48] XZ: Yes, I agree. That brings up two great points. Can you tell me a about how you think it can be done "correctly" [2013/01/24 12:48] XZ: In other words, what techniques [2013/01/24 12:48] XZ: are effective [2013/01/24 12:49] P1: to me instructors should use more than lecture to create trust and to teach effectively [2013/01/24 12:49] P1: the techniques in a virtual world could be using a simulation, collaborating with other students/universities for a larger learning environment [2013/01/24 12:50] XZ: Those are great, thank you. [2013/01/24 12:50] XZ: Secondly, the protection that is afforded from an avatar, do you think that helps in building swift trust, or do you think it is harder for trust to be established without the face to face relationship [2013/01/24 12:51] P1: by using voice and interactive components in a course or to establish a relationship, you actually can feel as if you are talking to the person f2f [2013/01/24 12:51] XZ: That is true [2013/01/24 12:52] P1: for instance, i recently attended a conference and met someone first time face-to-face that i have been interacting with in SL [2013/01/24 12:52] P1: I truly felt I knew the person and we chatted immediately, more so than others at the same conference that I met while there [2013/01/24 12:52] XZ: That is interesting, so you feel that the trust that was established in SL flowed over into RL? [2013/01/24 12:53] P1: yes i think so. [I]t is the same with students and faculty, they begin to trust that person and talk to them through office hours and the course material, virtual office hours that is [2013/01/24 12:53] XZ: I have seen that as well. [2013/01/24 12:53] XZ: Lastly, what would you say have been the outcomes of from building trust in virtual teams as an educator? [2013/01/24 12:54] P1: the students seem to do very well in the classes and [2013/01/24 12:54] P1: it has been my experience that they do better than some of our regular university classes [2013/01/24 12:55] P1: the instructors also tell me the averages of the students in SL are better than the averages in the physical classes, although they have not done an actual study [2013/01/24 12:55] XZ: That is a fascinating phenomenon [2013/01/24 12:55] XZ: Maybe due to the interactivity and immersive environment [2013/01/24 12:55] P1: i hope i can get someone to do an actual study	What does building trust do for you as an educator? I think that it helps us to communicate effectively and it also helps the students to be able to present their issues, thoughts, concerns, ideas, suggestions for improvement, and to negotiate better. I find that the groups I am a part of continue to work together - the longest group working together for over 4 years.

8	1/22/13 8:46AM	12	09:31] XZ: This friend request is to participate in a 30-40 minute interview in order to collect your story. Please let me know what date and time would be preferable for your participation. For more info on my research visit http://bit.ly/X9t0Xz[2013/01/18 09:32] XZ: I appreciate you taking the time to sign up for my study! Thanks [2013/01/22 08:46] P2: okay[2013/01/22 08:46] P2: tp me[2013/01/22 08:46] Second Life: Teleport offer sent to P2.[2013/01/22 08:46] XZ: Wonderful, Thank You [2013/01/22 08:48] P2: Here in SL I am enjoying learning lots of new things - scripting (badly) and creating photographs, machinima, musical things, teaching - enjoying it all and making lots of new friends. I live and work in Oxfordshire, UK, in the ICT advisory service - helping to educate teachers in making ICT enhance teaching and learning! [2013/01/22 08:49] P2: I am married and have a large family, Neil, Andrew, Phillip and Helen, plus partners and babies... and dogs![2013/01/22 08:56] P2: Typonese is my second language - in fact it stands a chance it is my first really ;-) What is your experience with building trust in virtual teams? Haven't thought about it, trust is a huge part of it, because people don't know me. Moodle and other non 3D environments. About safety and they know me, language lab and teach English, and there is no f2f relationship they come to the class and then come back and have built that relationship. Because they either like your style and what you are teaching or they don't come back. There are several students that I have that come to class religiously every week and won't miss it. And if they are they let me know. They have no obligation to choose me, but they do. How would you describe building trust in a virtual environment? Being honest and being who I am and laughing when necessary, and tell them if I know it and don't know it. Friendly open, not bothered if I don't know something, genuine	How did you know that trust had been built?You have to gentle, and laugh and act like you would in a real class room, getting used to period and once you get over it you just have fun. Having a little levity in the classroom is really good. If you can laugh and be yourself it helps with the learning experience. For instance, in about an hour and a half class we were talking about a Korenan dance so I dropped a dance script and in a few minutes we were all dancing in unison. The students loved it and were laughing. They were learning, and they won't forget that lesson because of the unique experiential experiences that you can have once you are used to this environment and working in this world. What was the effect of building trust in a virtual world on the learning environment?Trust is essential in this environment, because they don't know me. They don't have the f2f relationship to relate on. However, that can be a good thing, because the there isn't she is too old, or too tired or too slow is not a consideration. I am just a normal little avatar that looks much like other avatars, and look and speak much like any other teacher in any other classroom, virtual or not.
9	1/25/13 12:49PM	36	[12:49] P3: I we need to start with a definition of trust? Can you put that into perspective for me[12:50] XZ: Of course, I am speaking about the interpersonal bond between educator and student, which facilitates learning. [12:52] XZ: this study hopes to provide a foundation for educators to be able to identify ways in which a collaborative learning environment can be established through trust.[12:53] XZ: the purpose of this narrative study is to describe and present research that explains how the educator is undergoing a trust-building experience in virtual worlds that relates to positive group outcomes in the virtual team and ultimately generates a collaborative learning community.[12:53] P3: that word trust, is perhaps different between upper education and the K-12 industry, I just need to wrap my head around how you are using it[12:54] XZ: Yes, it is a very subjective term and means different things to different people. That is why I choose to do a qualitative analysis to identify the common themes among the stories[12:54] XZ: So I am really just interested in what it means to you and your experience with it...[12:55] P3: to me it means their ability to build relationships and collaborate to learn from each other[12:55] XZ: I am going under the assumption that building trust in a face to face classroom is different than building it virtually with avatars[12:55] XZ: Yes, that I trust you enough to take the information you give me as true[12:57] P3: I am always trying to teach my students to trust but verify especially when it comes to online[12:57] XZ: That is very important!	I have 5 different schools using SL out of my classes, the biggest difficulty was to get through the face to face interaction. I find that face to face interactions really serve to set the class up and the students expectations. They have a difficult time trusting since we are working in the K-12 environment. We are working to develop more resources for the remote learning and distance education. We want to be able to develop teleconference means to support on-line approaches, for instance it is difficult for their personalities to show through in the SL avatar form. Building that relationship is unique and depends on each student, and it is more difficult as an educator to get a sense for that without the F2F interaction. I feel that SL and the 3D context of virtual worlds is a natural progression for distance learning and the flipped classroom. It really requires us to look at the digital immigrants and how we are feeding into higher education. I try to get them to critically think and be active learners, I find that this facilitates learning among the group, and I as the educator just act as a moderator of sorts, offering advice and direction when needed, and working with the one's that need encouragement.

10	1/20/2013 9:05AM	35	XZ: Can you describe to me what is your experience with building trust? By trust...I mean the interpersonal bond between educator and student, which lends credibility and esteem to the educator[2013/01/20 09:12] P4: this is a question that I have not contemplated before your inquiry[2013/01/20 09:12] P4: so I tried to think about it and find its hard to explain[2013/01/20 09:13] XZ: yes it is[2013/01/20 09:13] P4: because I dont teach any differently here in virtual worlds, than I do in RL[2013/01/20 09:13] P4: this what I find interesting/strange about other faculty[2013/01/20 09:14] P4: they seems to think that we should use different strategies here[2013/01/20 09:14] P4: I suppose there are some, but not as many to me[2013/01/20 09:14] P4: so building trust here is the same as in RL[2013/01/20 09:14] XZ: That is very interesting to hear, because I am the same way...[2013/01/20 09:15] P4: oh, excellent[2013/01/20 09:15] XZ: Do you find that it is harder to build trust without the face to face interactions and non-verbal gestures?[2013/01/20 09:15] P4: no, I do not[2013/01/20 09:15] XZ: great[2013/01/20 09:16] P4: I seem to have a knack for finding the truth in ppl here[2013/01/20 09:16] P4: sometimes not as soon as I'd like but[2013/01/20 09:16] XZ: that is a great skill to have[2013/01/20 09:16] P4: I seem to route out the bad in ppl[2013/01/20 09:16] P4: I dont like it, but it happens[2013/01/20 09:17] XZ: So true, just like in the real world, bad seeds...[2013/01/20 09:17] XZ: everywhere[2013/01/20 09:17] P4: exactly[2013/01/20 09:17] XZ: ,What was the effect of building trust in a virtual world on the learning environment? [2013/01/20 09:17] XZ: So do you feel that the building of trust (interpersonal) is important to facilitate learning?[2013/01/20 09:20] P4: not so much learning as collaboration[2013/01/20 09:20] XZ: agreed[2013/01/20 09:21] P4: my students have to work together on assignments[2013/01/20 09:21] P4: so they must trust each other[2013/01/20 09:21] P4: and pull their own weight[2013/01/20 09:22] XZ: that is critical to having a successful outcome...so do you find that it is hard for them to build that trust with eachother in this environment?[2013/01/20 09:22] XZ: Or easier?[2013/01/20 09:22] XZ: or the same?[2013/01/20 09:22] P4: let me be clear, I think the virtual environment is an excellent teaching and learning platform[2013/01/20 09:22] P4: I dont' think its any different than F2F[2013/01/20 09:23] XZ: great[2013/01/20 09:23] P4: some ppl will argue that[2013/01/20 09:23] P4: most ppl, I suppose[2013/01/20 09:23] XZ: so you find that the same strategies work here as in F2F[2013/01/20 09:23] P4: most, yes[2013/01/20 09:23] P4: but I have not tried them all in either world[2013/01/20 09:24] P4: I advocate constructivisim in both worlds[2013/01/20 09:24] XZ: I see[2013/01/20 09:24] P4: student - centered[2013/01/20 09:25] XZ: so would you say that has helped with how the evelopment of trust evolved?[2013/01/20 09:25] P4: yes, for sure[2013/01/20 09:25] P4: I get to know my students and they get to know me first[2013/01/20 09:26] P4: I find out their interests first[2013/01/20 09:26] P4: then I build assignments around that[2013/01/20 09:26] P4: if my students are interested in what they are learning, they do better[2013/01/20 09:26] XZ: that is a great strategy for engagement![2013/01/20 09:26] XZ: yes they do[2013/01/20 09:26] P4: ty, it has worked for me[2013/01/20 09:27] XZ: what would you say have been the outcomes of from building trust in virtual teams as an educator?[2013/01/20 09:27] P4: virtual teams are more engaged[2013/01/20 09:27] P4: I think[2013/01/20 09:27] P4: and they build strong friendships[2013/01/20 09:27] P4: I think because they cant'[2013/01/20 09:27] P4: see each other in RL[2013/01/20 09:28] P4: they are more open and honest[2013/01/20 09:28] P4: some make friendships that last[2013/01/20 09:28] XZ: I have seen that myself as well[2013/01/20 09:28] P4: yes, many counselors using virtual worlds have told me the same[2013/01/20 09:28] XZ: It is very interesting to see the interaction that comes from it[2013/01/20 09:28] XZ: that is great[2013/01/20 09:28] P4: yes, it is - we laughed alot[2013/01/20 09:29] P4: had fun[2013/01/20 09:29] P4: that makes leanring much more	The pilot study we did in Second Life proved that having the right task was critical to the student's success. The task used required students to collaborate on the creation of a project charter document. In that instance, Second Life was merely used as a voice conferencing tool; participants used the voice chat feature but none of the other capabilities. 25) Second Life does not have support for shared text editors, therefore, participants used the audio chat feature to discuss the project charter while one person typed the information in a Word document. Based on this experience, it seemed that to build trust it was important to incorporate more of the features of Second Life. 26) On reflection, it is important to identify the most effective capabilities that correlate to increasing trustfulness and trustworthiness in virtual worlds. As one of my students pointed out, attending a lecture is not a good use of Second Life, but Second Life is great for interacting with others and for offering visual representations of ideas. Unlike real life, here, I can ban them from the island. I had an experience with a troubled one in SL, very disturbed individual, but not bad We think she is bipolar so I had to handle her differently: I had to give her special assignments she could handle and work one on one with her but that is the same in the face to face class

			enjoyable and retainable[2013/01/20 09:29] XZ: Yes it does![2013/01/20 09:29] P4: may ppl say this is a game[2013/01/20 09:29] P4: Ive never thought of it as that[2013/01/20 09:30] XZ: I get that all the time, and neither have I since I was introduced to it as an educational tool...but there is a lot to "serious gaming" for learning[2013/01/20 09:30] P4: oh, yes, indeed there is[2013/01/20 09:30] P4: I participated in a game MOOC, that was fascinating[2013/01/20 09:30] XZ: I much prefer this to the traditional asynchronous approach of distance learning[2013/01/20 09:31] XZ: I bet![2013/01/20 09:31] XZ: I think there is a lot of potential here[2013/01/20 09:31] P4: yes, I agree, me too[2013/01/20 09:31] P4: more potential than most professors are able to recognize[2013/01/20 09:31] P4: ppl either get this platform or they don'[2013/01/20 09:32] P4: there doesn't seem to be anyone in the middle[2013/01/20 09:32] XZ: I agree, it is a learning curve to it[2013/01/20 09:32] XZ: that is so true[2013/01/20 09:32] P4: for sure[2013/01/20 09:32] XZ: Well, again I want to thank you for taking the time to talk to me! Is there anything more you would like to add about trust in virtual worlds?[2013/01/20 09:32] P4: I spent a year learning the platform first before I taught here[2013/01/20 09:32] XZ: wow, that is great[2013/01/20 09:33] XZ: helps to have the familiarity[2013/01/20 09:33] P4: yes, that is what makes me angry about some educators[2013/01/20 09:33] P4: they come here to teach[2013/01/20 09:33] P4: and never learn how to really use the platform[2013/01/20 09:33] P4: they call themselves experts and they can barely sit in a chair[2013/01/20 09:34] XZ: very frustrating...I think that would definitely decrease my trust if I were their student[2013/01/20 09:34] P4: and they teach the way they do in RL, by lecture[2013/01/20 09:34] P4: indeed[2013/01/20 09:34] XZ: that would not work![2013/01/20 09:34] P4: it doesnt work, but more educators do that here than dont[2013/01/20 09:34] P4: they still think their old ways work[2013/01/20 09:35] XZ: that is interesting, I don't believe in that modality[2013/01/20 09:35] P4: their old ways dont work in F2F either[2013/01/20 09:35] XZ: I know it[2013/01/20 09:35] P4: and really, they dont care if their student learns the material or not[2013/01/20 09:35] XZ: I guess it will take time to transform the culture[2013/01/20 09:35] P4: Im speaking of the old ones[2013/01/20 09:35] XZ: Yes, I have seen much to much of that too.[2013/01/20 09:35] XZ: They only care about hearing themselves talk, and what the student does with it is not their problem[2013/01/20 09:36] P4: exactly[2013/01/20 09:36] XZ: takes all the fun out of teaching in my opinion[2013/01/20 09:36] P4: yes[2013/01/20 09:36] P4: they make me very angry[2013/01/20 09:36] P4: the ppl who are the most educated[2013/01/20 09:36] P4: the most intellegent are often the most closed minded	
11	1/25/13 12:49PM	38	34) XV: I am still trying to get voice settings back [2013/02/04 12:58] XV: one moment [2013/02/04 12:58] P5: seems like that makes two of us... just started up this computer [2013/02/04 12:59] XV: ok, brb I am going to try firestorm [2013/02/10 09:42] AO-HUD: 3623 bytes free [2013/02/10 09:42] #Firestorm LSL Bridge v2.3: <bridgeURL>http://sim4021.agni.lindenlab.com:12046/cap/00dd93bc-46c2-d55b-fc84-1ba2b0c653c5</bridgeURL><bridgeAuth>4f7e2581-1ffe-2ec6-a0c1-0b186f5c25d2</bridgeAuth><bridgeVer>2.3</bridgeVer> P5: it is very important to focus on what is in front of you at the moment, and you have to be clear about what your expectations are so that you can present that to the students clearly. You know you meet people in rl and you don't really know who they are initially either – it takes time whether it is in sl or rl. [17:58] P5: I do expect them to be "real"...... in my profession that's a loaded word, because we have layers of reality like an onion. But I read an interesting quote on someone's profile. I wish I could remember the author. It said something like..."Sometimes (I paraphrase) the friendships we make when we correspond are the most intimate ones." XV: so you feel that we build trust through our correspondence? P5: I would have to agree there. There is always the possibility of deception	In my study an important revelation was that among those who indicated they could not share trust here, they were also not very trusting in their real lives. Making the comparison between trust in virtual or real life was also recognized in several interviews. How do you developed trust with others in Second Life: Friendship, emotional support, and a willingness to help people find things and learn in the virtual world One of the consistent complaints I get from my students and faculty about functioning in SL is the learning curve when first arriving. Learning the basic functions, much less navigating hundreds of virtual land regions can be

			through writing. But there is also a veil that is lifted.... a certain type of inhibition we have when we speak f2f that is not there. P5: sometimes when we write, we say more what we would not say, because we are at a loss for words in real time. P5: And sometimes it doesn't matter if we never meet in the flesh. XV: as I was just about to ask... what you consider the benefits of the relationships you've experienced in SL? P5: A sense of comfort in being able to express more openly and more honestly in the virtual world because there is not a fear of consequences and this actually made it more real in a sense. My students have described ways of filtering information and of cautionary measures taken as they worked into relationships that they felt they could trust. Ultimately, for many, there was a very fine line between virtual and real.	overwhelming. With that also comes a sense of community and camaraderie. There are always residents that are experienced and will help others with questions they have.
			Director of the Upward Bound Math & Science Center at Penn State. Penn State UBMS serves eligible students from Philadelphia, Reading and Harrisburg school districts in Pennsylvania.	The purpose of the Upward Bound Math and Science Center (UBMS) at Penn State is to assist participating students in recognizing and developing their potential to excel in math or science and to encourage them to pursue postsecondary degrees in these fields.
				Educator and artist, loving adventure, exploring. and learning as in real life My art has taken me to many places in my imagination and in real life, and I present them for your pleasure
			[2013/01/16 09:22] Second Life: has given you this landmark: Clarence Hospital. School of Nursing Clinical Assistant Professor interested in developing Interprofessional (IPE) simulation and role play scenarios for senior nursing students.	Basically interested in teaching and learning in the virtual world environment.
			Senior Lecturer in Virtual Worlds	Education Innovation Centre University of the West of England
			Currently working for the Chicago Transit Authority, I am responsible for developing training programs for bus and rail operations employees.	I am a former teacher with the Chicago Public Schools
12	1/20/13 8:27	20	[2013/01/20 08:42] P6: PhD in Instructional Technology ~ Examined Engagement and Performance in SL. Specific interests include new media, emerging technologies, VWs, effective/efficient education & learning, 21st century education & learning. [2013/01/20 08:42] P6: For example, i trust you but this trust is really incurs no damage even if you were a bad person [2013/01/20 08:43] P6: so my trust, doesnt take much courage [2013/01/20 08:43] XV: so true, no risk really changes the dynamic a lot [2013/01/20 08:43] P6: but in vw [2013/01/20 08:43] P6: because of the freedom [2013/01/20 08:43] P6: there is a v gd friendship building aspect [2013/01/20 08:43] P6: and speed of testing things [2013/01/20 08:43] P6: so vw is gd for moving ahead quickly [2013/01/20 08:43] XV: I find that the social aspect helps with collaboration [2013/01/20 08:43] P6: if you know what you are testing [2013/01/20 08:44] P6: yes [2013/01/20 08:44] P6: its fun [2013/01/20 08:44] P6: vw must be fun for it to work [2013/01/20 08:44] P6: because unlike real life [2013/01/20 08:44] P6: its v limited [2013/01/20 08:44] XV: and is good for me since I work in Colorado and my colleagues are spread across the nation [2013/01/20 08:44] XV: It is [2013/01/20 08:44] P6: the information is v limited	• What is your experience with building trust in teams? P6: well, I think "trust" is too heavy a word here (in SL) because it doesn't incur any risk trust in a team, to me means, if you give some task or responsibility to a member, that they was able to carry it out properly without you having to watch over them. virtual worlds are not dangerous at all there is almost zero damage. XV: It is hard as an educator because we don't get that face to face bond with the student we have to establish our creditability other ways P6: its like talking on a telephone, the fact that the student decided that they want to learn and they don't have to choose the vw way but for whatever reasons they did, then they are really eager to learn to spend real life time to do something. Maybe they have a handicap - not meaning only in the physical sense - but time wise they could only learn through an online system so if you sound like a proper teacher and is

			[2013/01/20 08:44] P6: oh yes? how do you mean? [2013/01/20 08:44] P6: you only teach online? [2013/01/20 08:44] P6: no real face to face teaching? [2013/01/20 08:44] XV: It is a great substitute for face to face is that is not geographically possible [2013/01/20 08:44] XV: I do both [2013/01/20 08:45] XV: I like them both for different reasons [2013/01/20 08:45] P6: tell me a bit more? [2013/01/20 08:45] P6: what do you like about online teaching? [2013/01/20 08:45] XV: I prefer the face to face mode, but I do like that I can teach my students regardless of where they are [2013/01/20 08:45] P6: and what systems do you use for online teaching? [2013/01/20 08:45] XV: I have a lot of students in the military and they travel and move around a lot... [2013/01/20 08:46] P6: what subject do you teach? [2013/01/20 08:46] XV: This helps them to stay on track with their educational goals [2013/01/20 08:46] P6: its a great idea [2013/01/20 08:46] XV: I teach emerging media, web design, flash, etc... [2013/01/20 08:46] P6: online things itself [2013/01/20 08:46] XV: graphic design stuff [2013/01/20 08:46] XV: We use SL and Open SIm in addition to SLOODLE for the online content [2013/01/20 08:47] P6: yes these are v gd subjects for online [2013/01/20 08:47] P6: is there a campus here in sl? [2013/01/20 08:47] XV: I like the virtual world because it helps me to talk with them real time [2013/01/20 08:47] P6: you use live voice? [2013/01/20 08:47] XV: If bandwidth allows I do	offering clear instructions it means you are not some teenager trying to play teacher - Do you feel that they are more open to learning virtually or in a physical environment? I think learning in real life is the best - So offering clear instructions, much more rests on the communication in virtual worlds? learning in the virtual world - if its a subject specific to virtual worlds - for example building vw models etc. then it makes sense to do it in vw otherwise, its far better in real life XV: to establish that creditability, yes simulations are great here P6: only case where i have heard of an advantage is for Asperger syndromes, the Asperger people can perform without the handicap of having to decipher visual facial expressions and they could perform v well in sl XV: true P6: its an advantage for them XV: that is a very good point P6: this is the only case I have heard of XV: Do you think that it is important to trust the educator in these instances of vw learning? P6: which instances? XV: or do you think the student can be more self-taught regardless of the teacher in a virtual world class P6: its always better to have a teacher if you know what kind of help you need but its better in the real world and next, virtual world some people students cannot listen to instructions XV: so true P6: they learn much better through working out the problems themselves XV: that would be very difficult here P6: but the teacher is there to give guidance a go-to person

13			XV: What is your experience with building trust in virtual teams? P7: It is very regarding to the various communication channels that each VW can provide with its client viewer. Of course to have better results instantly you can organize all team before their introduction.	• How did you know that trust had been built? From my experience in should appeared even before students' introduction inside a VW • What was the effect of building trust in a virtual world on the learning environment? It was a great opportunity to get efforts from the VW, its tools that provide can help in various ways the communication of all users. • How would you describe building trust in a virtual environment? It's all about trust from the real world. I mean that if someone transferring an innovative knowledge field in VW, he/-she probably know other team members, but it is difficult to be understood if someone participating without considering other members. • What are your perceptions of how your development of trust evolved? There are involved simultaneously with the trust of real life, I cannot separate both of them. • Describe your experience with building trust in virtual worlds.I respect each member - with his thoughts or opinions - as a unique (cyber-) entity, and in this notion I follow a trail that consists the possible opportunities of collaboration and anticipated learning outcomes that becomes deeply from this process. • What have been the outcomes from building trust in virtual teams as an educator? Collaboration and respect of the "other" are the main twofold purpose of my courses.

Intertextual and Emplotment Data - left numbers & top letters used for analysis references

	H
14	University of Michigan Dearborn 10 John J. Cristiano, Co PI Director, Henry W. Patton Center for Engineering Education and Practice Dr. John J. Cristiano is the Director of the Henry W. Patton Center for Engineering Education and Practice (HP CEEP). The center was found in 1992 with support from Ford Motor Company and Chrysler with the mission is to be a leader in incorporating engineering practice, design, innovation and concepts of manufacturing technology at all levels of education by integrating the teaching environment with the world of practice. Since that time, the center has funded over 150 research projects involving 56 companies, over 120 students and 50 faculty. In addition, HP CEEP supports senior design projects in each of the four departments within the College of Engineering and Computer Science. Dr. Cristiano is responsible for stimulating and facilitating faculty research relationships, managing the partnerships between the university and industry with respect to the college's research and to facilitating the transfer and commercialization of Center developed technology. Prior to joining UM Dearborn, he served as the Assistant Director for the National Science Foundation Engineering Research Center for Reconfigurable Manufacturing Systems (ERC/RMS) and as an adjunct assistant professor at the University of Michigan. As an adjunct assistant professor, Dr. Cristiano taught the senior design course in the department of industrial and operations engineering, as well as courses on economic decision making, engineering modeling, and project management. The senior design course involved managing 10 to 15, student teams per term to solve industry problems. Projects can include topics such as inventory analysis and management, facilities layout, process simulation, workstation design and ergonomics, SQC,

	workflow analysis and design, database specifications, and TQM. Dr. Cristiano is a past winner of the Shingo prize for Excellence in Manufacturing Research and the 2000 INFORMS Technology Management Section Best Dissertation Award. He is published in Sloan Management Review, IEEE Transactions on Engineering Management, IEEE Transactions on Systems, Man, and Cybernetics, and Journal of Product Innovation Management. Dr. Cristiano holds a B.S.E. in computer engineering and M.S.E. and Ph.D. in industrial and operations engineering from the University of Michigan. Bruce R. Maxim, Co PI, Associate Professor, Computer and Information Science Dr. Bruce R. Maxim is Associate Professor of Computer and Information Science at the University of Michigan Dearborn. His research interests include: software engineering, human computer interaction, game design, artificial intelligence, and computer science education. He has published a number of papers on the animation of computer algorithms, game development, and educational computing applications. He is coauthor of a best-selling introductory computer science text and web content to support the world's most popular software engineering text. His recent research activities have been in the area of serious game development. Dr. Maxim is the architect of the ABET accredited Computer Science curriculum and the ABET-accredited Software Engineering curriculum at the University of Michigan Dearborn. He is creator of 15 Computer and Information Science courses dealing with software engineering, game design, artificial intelligence, user interface design, web engineering, software quality, and computer programming. He also serves as the faculty advisor to the local computing honor society (Upsilon Pi Epsilon). Dr. Maxim has supervised more than two hundred community based student software projects since 1997. The value of the software engineering work donated ranges from $40,000 to $80,000 per project and has created a great deal of good will in the community. Dr. Maxim began teaching game design courses at the University of Michigan Dearborn in 1999. His students have developed a large number of multimedia computer games. Several of these games were developed as collaborative projects between his students and digital animation students from the College of Creative studies in Detroit.
15	The next story is from the Bromley College of Further & Higher Education, based in the United Kingdom. This is Barry Spencer's experience with teaching an Object Oriented Programming Course: "I work in FE/HE in the UK and one of the courses I teach is OOP (Object Oriented Programming), and for the project this year, I decided to task my students with writing an application that would calculate the energy in Watts that could be extracted from the wind by a turbine. I started with a lecture on the basic physics involved, and then presented them with a formula, the idea being that they would be able to assimilate the various values (attributes) and any associated calculations into appropriate classes, and generally this has gone well. The next stage will be for them to code and test this in Java. Once the applications are working I will then send them of in a research kind of way, to place their devices, in an imaginary kind of way, at various locations across the UK for which average wind speeds are readily available, should be good. I had the thought, how about getting them to create a wind class that emulates the way in which wind can vary over time, as indeed it does? Then I thought, the wind blows in SL, so why not get them in world and have the experience of design/modeling? Of course the Java code will have to be translated into LSL, but as I found this is not a major problem really. Anyway I placed my own working version on a small islet kindly provided by Tony Lusch at Greenwich Maritime, thanks again for that Tony, and now its just a matter of waiting for the student turbine crop to grow. I see Second Life as offering a step change in social learning environments" (Spencer, 2009). Finally, Later Barry writes: "The unique qualities of 3-D virtual worlds can provide opportunities for rich sensory immersive experiences, authentic contexts and activities for experiential learning, simulation and role-play, modeling of complex scenarios, a platform for data visualization and opportunities for collaboration and co-creation that cannot be easily experienced using other platforms." (Spencer, 2009). Following is the excerpt on his project: "Bromley College is meeting the challenge of how to harness some of these opportunities for its students". **The activity** Using a patch of virtual land on an education island made available by a colleague at Greenwich University, Barry introduced Second Life to support the project work of two groups of 18/19 year-old students on Unit 25: Object Oriented Programming of the BTEC National Diploma for IT Practitioners Course. The course project involved the students: designing and coding programmed to calculate electricity generation of wind turbines; using the Second Life multi-user virtual environment to simulate the effect of 'real world' variables on turbines of different design and displaying the output of electricity generated; and evaluating their experience in Second Life. **The outcomes** Second Life allowed the students to see the scale of the turbines in relation to their virtual environment and this helped them to appreciate the amount of electricity they would generate in relation to their size. This **made explicit the real-life issues**, for example, "a very big turbine can't be put at the end of somebody's street or on their roof". Barry believes that access to this different way of conceptualizing a problem, together with the ability for students to interact with one another online, **promoted improved engagement** on this already-popular course. He compares the communication tools of a typical virtual learning environment (VLE) and those offered in multi-user environments such as Second Life. In a VLE, he suggests the individual learner remains essentially alone, whereas in Second Life, synchronous communication, identity and voice combine to offer "another level of virtual learning". The project also included end-of-course student surveys to help evaluate the learner experience of this use of Second Life (JISC RSC, 2009). In Second Life, the wind blows all the time, varying direction and speed. Using the live feeds in Second Life and variables such as location, time of the year and the force of the wind, the students were asked to write JAVA programmed to calculate how much electricity their turbines would generate. Barry Spencer says that this approach allowed the students "to see the problem". He also emphasizes the cross-curricular approach and simulation of real world activity, as benefits that use of Second Life in this context, afforded. The software development students in Second Life were able to model the operation of wind turbines in the physical world by varying the power of the wind and recording the corresponding change in electricity generation. Barry acknowledges the additional tuition that students needed in order to work in Second Life. Videos playing on a screen on the island showed these groups of students how to build the turbines with a simple introduction to the Linden Scripting Language (LSL), an event-driven programming language for building objects and specifying their behavior. For students familiar with JAVA programming, this proved to be a fairly straightforward activity, and Barry reports that two thirds of the group picked it up easily.
16	Second Life at Hong Kong Polytechnic University for Hotel and Tourism Management. Paul Penfold writes: "We used SL for orientation for 400 freshman students joining our Department. Started 3 weeks before the new semester, with 16 SL workshops in our computer lab first, then the last 2 weeks fully in SL. The program consisted of 7 individual learning activities: learning styles, multiple intelligences, active learning, academic

	honesty, classroom etiquette, citing references and hotel room design. Plus 3 competitions – parachuting, through the hoops and fashion show, and 8 live sessions on learning challenges, plagiarism, library and open Q&A finishing with a dance night and fashion show. We have been using a couple of chat bots to help with some of the activities and also employed some student helpers to assist and support students on a roster basis, so someone was always around from 9am to 9pm every day."
17	3D Library Visit: Using Second Life To Research Everyday Problems ScienceDaily () — Second Life is more than an on-line game for ETH Zurich. It is a handy three dimensional tool used for resolving real issues. ETH Zurich Computer Science students recently used it to analyze and solve the everyday frustrations involved in borrowing a book from a library. Full article: http://www.sciencedaily.com/releases/2008/03/080330225933.htm The project to tackle the problems that lending libraries face was carried out within the framework of the Information Systems Laboratory course taught by Professor Nesime Tatbul at the Computer Science Department (D-INFK), The study of information systems is a core area of computer science. It has evolved from the more established study of database management. Research into information systems now includes pervasive computing: the convergence of largely wireless technologies and the Internet. This may well signal a shift away from personal computing and into pools of shared information, available to anyone from anywhere at any time. Professor Tatbul's lab group used the ETH Zurich island in Second Life to visualize an automated library that uses Radio Frequency IDentification (RFID) technology. The virtual environment created in Second Life was the typical library setting: a check-out counter, a help desk, detection gates against theft and a self-check-in area. In reality, books were tagged with RFID labels and so were the ID cards of the library users. RFID readers were placed at the shelves, at a check-out counter, as well as at the library exit. There was, true to Second Life custom, the ever-hip female avatar, providing library presence. All that remained was to invite ETH Zurich's first virtual bookworm. The research group used five event detection queries to illustrate their system. For example, a book was checked in and checked out, a humdrum exercise that could lead to more than a bit of trouble if inaccuracies were recorded. And all libraries have trouble holding onto reference books that are restricted to internal use. Then there is the tendency to check out more than the allowed number of books on one subject, which is almost as great a problem as outright theft. All of these events reflect real life. Nevertheless, the researchers introduced some distinctively Second Life characteristics too, especially the way a book flew through space to be stuck on a wall after having been checked out properly. Three-tiered structure The system architecture of the Smart RFLib System is three-tiered. Its most important layer is data acquisition, the layer that interacts with the RFID tags on the books and on people via library cards. Electronic readers and antennas capture the data that itself is cleaned and compressed based on a time period or an event. The second tier – query processing – analyzes the collected information, detects important events of interest (theft, for example), and triggers the appropriate action or alert in response. This in turn updates the database, which then activates the third layer, visualization, which enables the viewer to see the results in three dimensions. It is essential that the data be clean, in other words, non-repetitive and always relevant. Although there are two data cleaning choices at the data acquisition layer, the adaptive method was chosen over the fixed-window alternative since it accommodates the uncertainty of data volume in a more flexible way. Sizing up the facts And size matters. RFID tag readers harvest huge amounts of data. To compress this deluge into fewer tuples (sequenced lists of objects), the project group developed two methods: regular responses to be sent by book-tags or data that are captured only when a tag acquires new information. Of course, solving one problem often creates another. In this case, the new challenge was getting the query-processing layer to talk to Second Life. There was a third difficulty as well: how to get Second Life to receive and process events from the real world. The normal client-server architecture for Second Life detects changes in the status or position of objects from the inside. Each object has its own script written in LSL, the Second Life programming language. Sophisticated though it is, Second Life is not able to capture all the information that one would like to keep track of concerning library books, people or policies. Therefore, the Informations Systems Lab students had to design an additional web interface to complement their Second Life visualizer. This interface enabled virtual visitors to make their own queries about books, check their current status as book borrowers and keep tabs on the system itself, all in real time. The SmartRFLib project team was able to use their five events to illustrate how well their approach worked. As well, they enjoyed being vigilant Second Life librarians: at the same time that one person was following the correct procedure in checking out a book, a maverick visitor tried to steal one. The alarm sounded. That test and others showed that the research team had achieved their goals; policy could be maintained and applied in their 3D library. Working with RFID was not easy, but the ETH Zurich Information Systems Lab project demonstrated that SmartRFLib could also be adapted to other RFID-based data management applications. Supply chain management, for example.
18	Differences in the development of trust and benevolence over the course of the study such that trust and benevolence increased among participants in the Game condition over the course of the project, but decreased among participants in the Chat condition. In other words, teams in the Game condition were able to develop a sense of trust in their teammates while trust fell and stagnated in the Chat condition. In both conditions, perceptions of ability and propensity to trust remained relatively constant over time. In the Game condition, perceptions of integrity rose over time while they fell in the Chat condition; however, this difference was not significant. Participants' propensity to trust remained relatively consistent in both conditions. From these results, we reject hypothesis 1 and accept hypothesis 2. Playing games with dynamic player roles does not significantly enhance perceptions of ability or integrity among members of a virtual team, though it does enhance perceptions of benevolence—a crucial component of trust acquisition (Jarvenpaa et al., 1998; Mayer et al., 1995). More importantly, playing games with dynamic player roles significantly enhances perceptions of trust among members of a virtual team. In sum, the results demonstrate that the teams in the Game condition developed more trust and were more inclined to perceive high levels of benevolence in their teammates than those in the Chat condition. The act of selecting the particular virtual tool, such as virtual worlds vice other collaboration tools, does not build trust or foster motivation within the team of student, rather it is educator's skills, which builds trust and may increase motivation. The selection of Second Life is only a channel for the facilitator of the virtual team to stimulate engagement from all the students.
19	The clarity, quality, and the richness of the transmission of the virtual communication will heavily influence the behavior of the students. Bruce R. Maxim from the University of Michigan-Dearborn posted the following story describing the work the UM-Dearborn is doing: "A key component of the University of Michigan-Dearborn's Metropolitan Vision is Student Engagement, an effort to help students to see the point of the knowledge they are acquiring-the real-world impact that their knowledge can achieve. Students can increase the impact of their talents by learning to work together, to lend their talents to the needs of their communities, and to achieve real passion for the fields of learning they are pursuing. This project is a core element in furthering our vision of student engagement." The College of Engineering and Computer Science at the University of Michigan-Dearborn (UM-Dearborn) is leveraging computing technology to

develop and build sustainable communities that bridge virtual and real worlds to address a pressing social problem through the use of college and high school students, the Second Life 3-D (SL) virtual world and the Food Bank Council of Michigan (FBCM).

Our general approach is for UM-Dearborn students to build a Campus of Hope that will provide a structure for future development. Students will work with the FBCM as a vehicle to build a community among their network of food banks, conceptualize the parameters of their problems (e.g. efficient distribution of canned goods), collaboratively develop and test solutions (e.g. minimal cost delivery route), and then implement the solution in the real world.

Initially, we are planning three projects to implement in Second Life for our community partner. The first will be the creation of a virtual food drive to educate people using the 3-D environment about how their donations travel through the system and reach people in need. The second will be the creation of a virtual exhibit showcasing the needs of the community partner and the benefits of collaboration in virtual worlds. The third will be the creation of facilities to support meetings held jointly in real life and second life.

Campus of Hope: Using the Virtual World to Improve Our World Principal Investigators: John J. Cristiano Bruce R. Maxim, Director, Henry W. Patton Associate Professor, Center for Engineering Education and Practice Computer and Information Science, Email: cristiano@umich.edu Email: bmaxim@umich.edu, Phone: 313 593 0941 Phone: 313 436 9155 Campus of Hope: Using the Virtual World to Improve Our World, University of Michigan Dearborn 1 INTRODUCTION AND PROJECT SUMMARY A key component of the University of Michigan-Dearborn's Metropolitan Vision is Student Engagement, an effort to help students to see the point of the knowledge they are acquiring—the real-world impact that their knowledge can achieve. Students can increase the impact of their talents by learning to work together, to lend their talents to the needs of their communities, and to achieve real passion for the fields of learning they are pursuing. This project is a core element in furthering our vision of student engagement. The College of Engineering and Computer Science at the University of Michigan-Dearborn (UM-Dearborn) is proposing to leverage computing technology to develop and build sustainable communities that bridge virtual and real worlds to address a pressing social problem through the use of college and high school students, the Second Life® 3-D (SL) virtual world and the Food Bank Council of Michigan (FBCM). Second Life® is a 3-D virtual world that is created by its online participants (Residents). Since opening to the public in 2003, it has grown explosively and as of today is inhabited by millions of Residents from around the globe. It is a global community working together to build a new online space for creativity, collaboration, commerce, and entertainment. It strives to bridge cultures; welcomes diversity, values free expression, compassion and tolerance are the foundation for community in this new world. Virtual worlds are equipped with social networking facilities and online collaboration tools (integrating blogs, personal homepages and sometimes VoIP), which transformed them into highly valuable tools for e-learning and distance collaboration. Our general approach is for UM-Dearborn students to build a Campus of Hope that will provide a presence for the Ford Motor Company Fund in Second Life and provide a structure for future development. The structure of the campus will be aligned with the pillars of community involvement. In addition, students will work with the FBCM as a vehicle to build a community among their network of food banks, conceptualize the parameters of their problems (e.g. efficient distribution of canned goods), collaboratively develop and test solutions (e.g. minimal cost delivery route), and then implement the solution in the real world. Initially, we are planning three projects to implement in Second Life for our community partner. The first project is the implementation of a toolbox that would allow people from a network of food banks to plan and optimize food pickup and delivery routes. A second would be the creation of a virtual food drive to educate people using the 3-D environment about how their donations travel through the system and reach people in need. The third would be the creation of a virtual exhibit showcasing the needs of the community partner and the benefits of collaboration in virtual worlds. The use of a virtual property or island as an engineering test bed has number of benefits. It allows geographically diverse stakeholders to interact with each other in real-time while working on a problem. The virtual island also serves as problem solution repository that can be used as case studies by educators and manipulated by stakeholders as parameters change. The virtual island can also be used to help build community awareness of the problems facing the community partner as it tries to complete its mission. The virtual environment may also serve to provide a realistic face on the people served by food banks in our state and create feelings of empathy on the part of its visitors. USING THE VIRTUAL WORLD - INNOVATIVE APPROACH TO "BUILDING SUSTAINABLE COMMUNITIES" The Ford College Community Challenge uses the term "Sustainable Communities" to describe healthy, livable communities that are poised to thrive in a global economy, encompassing a wide range of issues, from education to safety to mobility to arts and culture. To realize this goal, people from diverse backgrounds, regions and generations must have the ability to organize, collaborate, and exchange information on a broad scale in order to learn how to make a difference in their own community. To address that challenge, UM-Dearborn is proposing to create the Campus of Hope in the three-dimensional virtual community of Second Life that is created entirely by its members or residents (see Attachment D for more information). The Campus of Hope will provide an environment that will facilitate the social networking of organizations with common missions centered on the pillars of community activity that are the focus of the Ford Motor Company Fund. The creation of this platform will enable the UM-Dearborn vision of building of communities on multiple levels (high schools, universities, community organizations, and industry) and in multiple dimensions (both the virtual and real worlds) to make a tangible difference. In addition, this project provides a vehicle for educating high school and college students in science and engineering while they work to address a pressing social need. Campus of Hope: Using the Virtual World to Improve Our World University of Michigan Dearborn 2 The proposed strategy is two-fold: (1) Develop an initial presence in Second Live that provides a framework for future detailed development over time by future student teams. This would include basic information for key local community organizations that are consistent with each of the Ford Motor Company Fund pillars. For example the American Heritage wing might include The Henry Ford, the Detroit Institute of Art and the Detroit Symphony Orchestra etc.; (2) In the Community Initiatives wing, students will create a fully functional environment to address the pressing social need of hunger in our state. The 3-D virtual world developed by students will allow food banks across the State of Michigan to collaborate, exchange of best practices, and access tools and resources for optimizing their operations. The goal is for solutions developed and piloted in the virtual world (e.g., truck routing simulations) to be implemented in the real world. Donors, government officials, industry partners can visit the site to better learn about the issues, challenges, and operations of food banks by being immersed in the environment. Virtual conferences can be held in the Campus of Hope classroom involving food banks around the nation and world further extending the community. New and innovative methods (e.g., virtual food drive) will be developed to engage and broaden volunteer participation, and ultimately to increase the ability to raise funds and distribute food to those in need. Figure 1: Campus of Hope – The Ford Motor Company Fund Presence in Second Life A STUDENT DRIVEN PROJECT The engine of this project and future development in Second Life will be the Senior Design teams primarily from the department of

Computer and Information Science (CIS), with other departments within the College of Engineering and Computer Science (CECS) participating as their expertise is required. The student team members, not the faculty advisor, manage these teams. The CIS capstone design experience is offered as two, two credit-hour courses which students complete over two semesters (eight months) and is required of all CIS majors (software engineering, computer science, and information systems). The CIS senior design course has a long tradition of working with community-based partners. Dr. Maxim has supervised more than two hundred community-based student software projects since 1997. The dollar value of the software engineering work donated ranges from $40,000 to $80,000 per project and has created a great deal of good will in the community. This proposal is a logical extension of that tradition and provides a vehicle for future teams to build upon this work but to maximize their impact on the community beyond a single partner. Student Project Manager and Development Team A Graduate Student Research Assistant (GSRA) will be hired using the project funds to direct the work of establishing the Second Life Island. Two part-time student programmers and a part-time student graphic artist will assist the GSRA. This student team will serve as resources to both the community partner and the senior design teams to ensure a timely and quality solution is developed. This group will be responsible for the roll out and training of the FBCM and their network of food banks. This will be accomplished through both on-site visits and centrally held meetings. Senior Design Teams CECS senior design teams will be tasked with defining, developing, and implementing the solutions to the client's problems. In general, students work in three-or-four person teams with in the mutually agreed upon project defined with the sponsor. Once project teams assemble, class meetings consist of seminar-type class discussions on professional issues and team presentations of significant project milestone artifacts. In addition to the two hours of class-time each week, students put in at least six hours per week out-of-class on their project. The out-of-class time in the capstone course consists of team meetings, project planning, software design, product implementation, Campus of Hope: Using the Virtual World to Improve Our World University of Michigan Dearborn 3 presentation preparation, report writing, meeting with clients, and consultation with instructor. The six hours of outside work is very important as a means of fostering team development. The capstone projects generally require about 500 hours of student effort to complete Figure 2: Student Teams Drive the Building of Communities The role of the faculty in our course is that of a coach or mentor not a project manager. The students handle routine client contact. Project scheduling and progress tracking is also handled by the student teams. The instructor is available to help student teams resolve unusual problems with the project and the client. The instructor provides feedback on the milestone documents and presentations. A final presentation is required of all teams at the end of the second semester and includes a product demonstration and report. Students must present a letter of acceptance from their client to the instructor in order to receive a grade. The use of the client acceptance letter is a very important element of our course to drive home to students the importance of satisfying their clients' needs. High School Student Participation This project offers the opportunity to build a sense of community with students that extends beyond the campus population. To stimulate relationships between university and high school students and between high school students from diverse backgrounds, we will host a series of 3 one-day events where we will bring high school students to campus to work together on the issue of hunger in our state. A diverse group of high school students (~30) will be invited to participate from our Detroit Area Pre-College Engineering Program (DAPCEP) as well as our Ford Partnership for Advanced Studies Program (PAS). Students participating in this program will work with UM-Dearborn students to become familiar with both the challenges and operations of the Food Bank Council of Michigan, science and engineering, and the virtual environment of Second Life. The goal of this activity is to forge friendships among the diverse group of students through their use of science and engineering to assist people in need, and indoctrinating them into a culture of community service. AN URGENT AND UNMET COMMUNITY NEED It is well documented that the State of Michigan facing extremely difficult times and in particular the need for vital assistance. The food banks have seen a 20% increase in the need for food assistance. Since 2003 the number of Michigan households receiving food stamps has increased 53%. One in five Michigan children under 18 are in a household qualifying for assistance. Food stamps provide assistance but it [sic] does not provide all of a families [sic] needs for food. These numbers are for those who qualify for food stamps, the difficulty is that many people do not qualify for food stamps in our state and they are the ever-increasing number of the working poor. People, who have full time jobs, make too much money for assistance but cannot make ends meet due to the rising cost of food and fuel. These are the families that are truly vulnerable and need our assistance. It has been difficult for food banks to meet the rising need in the state of Michigan due to the struggling economy and a decrease in donations. The FBCM and its members are looking for new partnerships to assist us in the growing need of feeding those that are hungry in our state. Campus of Hope: Using the Virtual World to Improve Our World University of Michigan Dearborn 4 Figure 3: A Community of Communities Focused on Alleviating Hunger in Michigan THE FOOD BANK COUNCIL OF MICHIGAN - A COMMUNITY-BASED PARTNER The University of Michigan-Dearborn is pleased to be partnering with the Food Bank Council of Michigan (FBCM) for the initial detailed development on the Campus of Hope in Second Life. The mission of the FBCM is to provide statewide leadership to food banks in their efforts to alleviate hunger through the efficient distribution of food to those in need. The FBCM is made up of member regional food banks. The regional food banks, along with their subsidiary distribution organizations and branch warehouses, safely store and provide millions of pounds of surplus vegetables, fruits and other grocery items to more than 2500 local agencies serving each of the 83 counties in Michigan. The FBCM also provides a central, single voice to address the issue of hunger. They educate and advocate about the need for food and food security for everyone. Food security is defined by the United States Department of Agriculture as: access by all people at all times to enough food for an active, healthy life. Food banks rely on donated surplus food to stock their shelves. The food may be free, but there is considerable cost to transport it into and around the state. Transportation is the single, largest expense in operating a food bank. While Michigan food banks have access to donated product from all over the country, the costs associated with getting the product here can be a barrier to families receiving assistance. CAMPUS INVOLVEMENT This project will primarily will be an interdisciplinary project involving students from the four departments (see Figure 2) within the College of Engineering and Computer Science (CECS) as necessary. Initially, the project will primarily involve student teams from the Computer and Information Science and Industrial and Manufacturing Systems Engineering. In addition, the team will require a graphic/industrial design person who will likely come from the College of Arts, Sciences, and Letters (CASL). LEVERAGING EXISTING RESOURCES The UM-Dearborn has agreed to waive the indirect costs normally charged for projects of this type. This means that the entire award amount will be available to support the project activities. This equivalent to a $30K contribution to the project by UM-Dearborn. In addition, the Henry W. Patton Center for Engineering Education and Practice (HP-CEEP) agrees to continue to cover the cost of the property in Second Life for a period of 4 additional years ($10K value). Also, Campus of Hope: Using the Virtual World to Improve Our World University of Michigan Dearborn five each term HP-CEEP also provides grants to support the activities of CECS senior design project teams which will provide an extra $5K in funding for

	this project. In addition to the financial resources identified, relationships will be leveraged with DAPCEP, the Ford PAS program, as well as our many industry collaborators who may be able to assist with the issues facing the FBCM. SUSTAINABILITY OF THE PROJECT The CIS department has required senior design students to work on team-based software development projects with external clients since 1995 and plans to continue this practice for the foreseeable future. In addition, HP-CEEP will continue to pay the Second Life costs of maintaining the island for four years following the conclusion of the funding period so the development of the Campus of Hope will continue until at least 2013. The task of maintaining existing applications will be handled by enlisting the support of students from the UM-Dearborn chapter of Upsilon Pi Epsilon (UPE). Dr. Maxim serves as its faculty adviser. EXTENDING THE LIFE OF THE INITIATIVE The investigators are actively investigating funding sources to allow CIS senior design students to work with K-12 teachers and high school students to create educational game software to assist in the delivery of subject matter material. Games can be used to change attitudes, beliefs, and behaviors. Games can stimulate creativity and innovation on the part of their players. Role-playing games can help build players social skills. Virtual reality games can foster learning history and cultural heritage. Immersive game environments can be used to build players' knowledge and skills. PUBLICITY/COMMUNICATION PLAN The recognition of this project and support from the Ford Motor Company Fund will take multiple forms, using both traditional and non-traditional communication channels to raise awareness and reach the largest audience. These are summarized in Figure 4. Note that all public releases pertaining to the Ford Motor Company Fund will be mutually agreed upon. Figure 4: The Publicity and Communication Plan use both Traditional and Non Traditional Approaches The key aspects of the publicity and communication plan lie in the non-traditional methods to be used. In particular, the access to information and the availability of "virtual gifts" that can be distributed in Second Life reach a large audience. A conference will be held simultaneously on campus and in Second Life entitled "Using a Virtual World to Improve our World". The purpose of this conference is to showcase the projects and publicize the needs and accomplishments of our community partner. It would be our hope to stimulate other people to undertake similar partnerships using resources from the real world and virtual worlds like Second Life.

APPENDIX D: KEYWORD LIST AND NOTES

	I			J	K			L
	Word	**Count**	**Weighted %**	**Similar Words**	**Word**	**Count**	**Weighted %**	**Similar Words**
20	learning	213	1.02	acquisition, check, checked, condition, conditions, hear, hearing, instructions, know, knowledge, learn, learned, learning, learns, read, see, seeing, sees, studies, study, take, takes, taking, teach, teaching, watch, watching	chuckles	5	0.04	chuckles
21	see	167	0.66	attend, attended, attending, catch, check, checked, consider, considering, control, date, encounter, experience, experiences, fancy, find, finding, findings, look, looking, looks, meet, meeting, meetings, project, projects, realize, regarding, see, seeing, sees, view, visit, visiting, visual, watch, watching	component	5	0.03	component, components, element, elements, factor
22	get	163	0.54	arriving, becomes, becoming, begin, begins, bring, bringing, brings, catch, come, comes, develop, developed, development, find, finding, findings, generates, get, getting, going, having, incur, incurs, let, lets, letting, make, makes, making, received, start, started, stimulate, take, takes, taking	computer	5	0.04	computer
23	trust	144	1.2	believe, commitments, committed, hope, hopefully, hoping, hopes, sure, trust, trusted, trustfulness, trusting	each other	5	0.04	each other
24	work	134	0.66	act, bring, bringing, brings, exercise, exercises, form, functioning, functions, going, influence, make, makes, making, play, played, playful, playing, process, run, shape, shapes, studies, study, turn, work, worked, working, works	either	5	0.04	either
25	experience	115	0.43	experience, experienced, experiences, feel, feelings, get, getting, having, know, live, lives, received	everyone	5	0.04	everyone
26	comprehend	112	0.01	comprehend	feature	5	0.04	feature, features, having
27	educator	101	0.65	develop, developed, development, educated, education, educational, educator, educators, instructions, school, schools,	fire	5	0.02	fire, light, lighting, lights, terminals

				teach, teaching, training				
28	second	101	0.76	back, bit, instantly, minute, minutes, moment, sec, second, secondly	force	5	0.02	force, pull, push
29	immersive	90	0.01	immersive	full	5	0.02	full, richness
30	virtual	90	0.8	almost, nearly, virtual, virtually	generates	5	0.01	author, generates, product, sources
31	emotional	89	0.01	emotional	got	5	0.04	got
32	building	88	0.56	build, building, builds, establish, established, establishing, flesh, form, make, makes, making, progression, shape, shapes	grey	5	0.04	grey
33	good	84	0.31	dear, dependency, depends, effect, effective, effectively, effects, experts, full, good, honest, honestly, nearly, respect, right, safe, secure, serious, skill, skills, sound, sounds, well	head	5	0.02	gallery, head, leading
34	life	84	0.7	animated, life, live, lives	imagine	5	0.04	imagine, resource, resources
35	make	83	0.23	brand, clear, clearly, create, establish, established, establishing, form, give, giving, having, hit, hold, holding, make, makes, making, name, ready, realize, take, takes, taking	increase	5	0.02	increase, increased, increases, increasing, progression
36	creativity	78	0.01	creativity	indicate	5	0.01	indicate, indicated, suggest, suggested, suggestions
37	students	72	0.64	student, students, students'	initiate	5	0.01	initially, initiate, installed, knowledge
38	take	72	0.21	accept, accepted, bring, bringing, brings, carry, charter, choose, conduct, conducting, consider, considering, contains, direct, direction, engaged, engagement, exactly, guide, having, hold, holding, leading, read, removed, return, select, selecting, selection, submit, take, takes, taking, training, win	integrity	5	0.04	incorporate, incorporating, integrity, structured
39	face	69	0.39	aspect, aspects, case, cases, express, expressed, expression, expressions, face, front, line, look, looking, looks, present, presentation	interpersonal	5	0.04	interpersonal
40	think	63	0.38	believe, consider, considering, guess, imagine, mean, meaning, means, reason, reasons, remember, suppose, think, thinking, thought, thoughts	left	5	0.04	left, remained
41	world	63	0.51	creation, domain, global, public, publication, reality, universities, university, world,	line	5	0.02	channel, channels, contrast, line

				worlds, worldwide				
42	entered	60	0.4	entered, introduced, participant, participants, participants', participate, participated, participating, participation	made	5	0.04	made
43	just	59	0.36	barely, exactly, good, hard, just, merely, right	may	5	0.04	may
44	real	57	0.37	actual, actuality, actually, genuine, material, materials, real, reality, really	new	5	0.04	new
45	already	56	0.01	already	notice	5	0.01	card, notice, post, posted
46	settings	56	0.3	adjust, adjusting, background, context, correctly, fit, limited, limits, local, located, location, locations, lot, mark, place, positive, put, ready, set, sets, setting, settings	old	5	0.03	old, previously
47	going	52	0.13	break, extending, fit, going, last, lastly, leading, live, lives, loss, move, moving, run, sound, sounds, start, started, tour, travel, turn	permissions	5	0.02	allow, allowed, allows, permissions
48	like	52	0.39	care, compare, correspond, like, potential, probably, wish	prompt	5	0.01	prompt, quickly, suggest, suggested, suggestions
49	means	52	0.22	averages, based, close, closed, hate, important, importantly, mean, meaning, means, significance, significant, significantly, way, ways	qualitative	5	0.04	qualitative
50	yes	52	0.46	yes	read	5	0.01	indicate, indicated, read, version
51	give	50	0.17	afforded, break, commitments, committed, establish, established, establishing, feed, feeding, generates, gifts, give, giving, hand, open, openly, present, presentation, render, rendering, return, spring	received	5	0.02	having, received, welcome
52	used	50	0.38	enjoy, enjoyable, exercise, exercises, functioning, functions, habits, purpose, roles, use, used, useful, using	responsibility	5	0.01	responsibility
53	delightful	48	0.41	delightful, enjoy, enjoyable, please, revelation	revealed	5	0.02	break, reveal, revealed, revelation
54	teams	48	0.43	team, teams	session	5	0.04	session, sit
55	place	47	0.16	commitments, committed, direct, direction, local, located, location, locations, office, place, point, pointed, points, positive, post, posted, properties, put, send, sending, site, space, spaces, station	sit	5	0.02	model, models, ridings, sit
56	colleagues	45	0.01	colleagues	sorry	5	0.02	blue, sorry
57	know	45	0.15	bed, know, knowledge, love, loved, recognize, recognized, wise	stay	5	0.01	check, checked, stay, stopped

58	want	45	0.26	lack, miss, missed, need, needed, needing, needs, private, require, required, requires, want, wish	stored	5	0.04	memory, stored
59	need	44	0.13	ask, involved, involves, motivation, need, needed, needing, needs, require, required, requires, take, takes, taking	tab	5	0.03	check, checked, tab
60	offer	44	0.3	extending, going, offer, offered, offering, offers, provide, providing, volunteers	testing	5	0.02	run, screen, test, testing
61	participate	44	0.19	active, activities, activity, engaged, engagement, involved, involves, participant, participants, participants', participate, participated, participating, participation, player	texture	5	0.04	texture, textures
62	class	43	0.26	class, classes, course, courses, form, separate, sorts, year, years	two	5	0.04	two
63	benefits	42	0.01	benefits	walk	5	0.04	walk
64	feel	41	0.12	feel, feelings, look, looking, looks, notion, opinion, opinions, sense, touch	wrap	5	0.03	cloth, clothes, wrap, wrapping
65	help	40	0.29	available, facilitate, facilitates, facilitator, facilitators, help, helped, helpful, helping, helps, portion, serve, support, supporter	academic	4	0.04	academic
66	find	38	0.12	bump, encounter, feel, feelings, find, finding, findings, happening, happens, notice	ahead	4	0.02	ahead, forward, leading
67	first	38	0.2	begin, begins, first, initially, initiate, low, start, started	analysis	4	0.04	analysis
68	thank	38	0.32	appreciate, thank, thanks	anyone	4	0.04	anyone
69	emphasize	37	0.01	emphasize	aoc	4	0.04	aoc
70	great	37	0.29	capital, expect, expectations, great, heavy, large, neat	aspect	4	0.01	aspect, aspects, view
71	look	37	0.11	appeared, bet, dependency, depends, expect, expectations, look, looking, looks, seem, seemed, seems, sound, sounds, wait, waiting	assumption	4	0.03	assumption, suppose
72	come	36	0.14	amount, approach, approaches, becomes, becoming, come, comes, decent, follow, followed, following, seeds, seem, seemed, seems	Blob	4	0.04	blob
73	point	36	0.09	channel, channels, design, direct, direction, guide, head, indicate, indicated, item, items, levels, orient, oriented, period, point, pointed, points, show, shows, stopped	block	4	0.02	block, forget, stopped, stuff
74	open	35	0.12	capabilities, clear, clearly, initially, initiate, open,	brand	4	0.01	brand, mark, post, posted

				openly, possibility, possible, spread, subject, subjective, subjects				
75	chat	34	0.27	chat, chatted, visit, visiting	brb	4	0.04	brb
76	hold	34	0.09	appreciate, carry, check, checked, contains, control, entertaining, handle, having, hold, holding, moderate, moderator, obligation, properties, retainable, support, supporter, wait, waiting	bridge	4	0.04	bridge
77	study	33	0.1	consider, considering, contemplated, field, reported, studies, study, subject, subjective, subjects, survey	carry	4	0.01	carry, post, posted, run
78	describe	32	0.17	describe, described, describing, identify, key, line, name, reported	center	4	0.01	center, centered, focus, sum
79	patience	32	0.01	patience	cited	4	0.02	cited, mentioned, quote, quotes
80	tell	32	0.16	evident, narrative, order, relate, relates, relatively, reveal, revealed, separate, several, tell, telling	cloth	4	0.01	cloth, clothes, material, materials
81	including	31	0.01	including	consistent	4	0.02	body, consistent, consists
82	keep	31	0.1	continue, continued, hold, holding, keep, live, lives, retainable, save, saved, support, supporter	correlate	4	0.01	correlate
83	name	31	0.11	assign, assignments, call, called, cited, design, identify, list, mentioned, name	country	4	0.01	country, land, nation
84	region	31	0.25	area, part, region, regions	creditability	4	0.01	cited, creditability, mentioned
85	secondlife	31	0.28	secondlife	dance	4	0.04	dance, dancing
86	Trying	31	0.2	attempt, efforts, hear, hearing, proved, render, rendering, test, testing, tried, try, trying	design	4	0.01	design, innovative, plans
87	Meet	30	0.09	encounter, fit, gather, meet, meeting, meetings, play, played, playful, playing, received, touch	document	4	0.02	document, paper
88	Much	30	0.22	lot, much, often	dropped	4	0.02	dropped, miss, missed, spend
89	Outcomes	30	0.16	consequence, effect, effective, effectively, effects, events, outcome, outcomes, results, terminals	easier	4	0.01	easier
90	Time	30	0.27	clip, time, times	engagement	4	0.01	engaged, engagement, mesh
91	Environment	29	0.26	environment, environments	enhance	4	0.04	augmenting, enhance, enhances
92	Established	28	0.09	administration, administrators, based, demonstrate, establish, established, establishing, found, installed, natural, naturally, organization, organize, proved, show, shows, valid	fell	4	0.03	dropped, fell, flying

93	One	28	0.25	one, ones, single	functioning	4	0.01	functioning, functions, perform, serve
94	Cohesive	27	0.01	cohesive	gave	4	0.04	gave
95	Different	27	0.24	difference, differences, different, differently, otherwise, unlike	handicap	4	0.02	check, checked, handicap
96	Interview	27	0.21	audience, interview, interviews, question, questions	icon	4	0.04	icon, icons
97	Present	27	0.1	awards, currently, delivered, demonstrate, display, displayed, introduced, introduction, present, presentation, show, shows, soon, submit	implications	4	0.01	implications, suggest, suggested, suggestions
98	Really	27	0.11	actual, actuality, actually, genuine, really, truly	inclined	4	0.02	inclined, list, run, tend
99	Show	27	0.08	appeared, display, displayed, evident, express, expressed, expression, expressions, proved, read, registered, render, rendering, screen, show, shows, view	Invite	4	0.02	invite, received
100	Teach	27	0.07	command, instructions, teach, teaching	Later	4	0.04	later
101	Completed	26	0.13	accomplish, close, closed, completed, completion, end, ended, finish, realize, terminals	lindenlab	4	0.04	lindenlab
102	Now	26	0.16	direct, direction, immediately, instantly, now, present, presentation, today	lost	4	0.02	lost, maze, miss, missed
103	Online	26	0.23	online	lsl	4	0.04	lsl
104	Project	26	0.11	design, plans, project, projects, task, tasks	mac	4	0.04	mac
105	talk	26	0.23	lecture, speak, speaking, talk, talking, talks, verbal	machine	4	0.02	machine, organization, organize
106	effect	25	0.07	accomplish, effect, effective, effectively, effects, establish, established, establishing, force	many	4	0.04	many
107	finish	25	0.1	close, closed, culture, end, ended, final, finish, goal, goals, last, lastly, stopped, terminals	middle	4	0.01	center, centered, middle
108	game	25	0.12	back, game, games, gaming, play, played, playful, playing	mistrust	4	0.01	mistrust
109	possible	25	0.15	hypothesis, maybe, perhaps, possibility, possible, potential	object	4	0.04	object
110	well	25	0.11	advantage, comfort, comfortable, consideration, intimate, well	off	4	0.02	hit, off', removed
111	avatar	24	0.21	avatar, avatars	often	4	0.03	frequency, frequently, often
112	course	24	0.1	course, courses, feed, feeding, flowed, flowing, line, natural, naturally, run, track	particular	4	0.02	particular, picky, special, specific
113	ideas	24	0.14	idea, ideas, mind, minded, themes, thought, thoughts	phoenix	4	0.04	phoenix

114	information	24	0.14	conversation, conversational, data, info, information, instructions, intimate, sources	psychological	4	0.01	psychological
115	perceptions	24	0.13	appreciate, insights, notice, perceptions, sense	public	4	0.01	advertisements, public, publication
116	TRUE	24	0.15	dependency, depends, genuine, honest, honestly, right, true, truth	push	4	0.02	advertisements, buttons, push
117	voice	24	0.17	part, sound, sounds, voice	recognized	4	0.01	realize, recognize, recognized
118	condition	23	0.09	check, checked, condition, conditions, consideration, shape, shapes, status, term, terms, training, weather	reminds	4	0.03	monitor, prompt, reminds
119	develop	23	0.11	break, develop, developed, development, evolve, evolved, evolves	risk	4	0.03	dangerous, risk
120	let	23	0.1	allow, allowed, allows, let, lets, letting	seen	4	0.04	seen
121	perspective	23	0.01	perspective	shaders	4	0.04	shaders
122	playing	23	0.06	act, bet, perform, play, played, playful, playing, roleplay, run, turn	Social	4	0.04	social
123	resident	23	0.2	resident, residents, rests	Step	4	0.03	measures, step
124	example	22	0.11	case, cases, example, exercise, exercises, instance, instances, lesson, model, models	strategies	4	0.04	strategies, strategy
125	teleport	22	0.2	teleport	technology	4	0.03	technical, technology
126	app	21	0.19	app	Text	4	0.01	text
127	better	21	0.17	best, better, break, improvement, improving	Three	4	0.04	three
128	interesting	21	0.14	concerns, interest, interested, interesting, interests, involved, involves, worries	traditional	4	0.01	traditional
129	person	21	0.17	individual, individuals, person, personal, personalities, personally, someone	ultimately	4	0.03	final, ultimately
130	ways	21	0.09	direct, direction, mode, room, style, way, ways	unique	4	0.04	unique
131	able	20	0.16	able, capabilities	upload	4	0.04	upload, uploaded, uploading
132	coach	20	0.16	coach, management, training	user	4	0.04	user, users
133	detail	20	0.11	detail, detailed, details, item, items, particular, point, pointed, points	verify	4	0.02	control, valid, verify
134	important	20	0.08	consequence, crucial, implications, important, importantly, moment, significance, significant, significantly	vertex	4	0.04	vertex
135	start	20	0.04	begin, begins, initially, initiate, jump, part, start, started	within	4	0.03	inside, within
136	agent	19	0.17	agent, factor	wow	4	0.04	wow
137	agree	19	0.1	agree, agreed, check, checked, correspond, fit, hold, holding	www	4	0.03	web, www

138	beyond	19	0.01	beyond	added	3	0.02	added, adding, advertisements
139	even	19	0.11	equally, even, evening, levels, regular, regularly, still, yet	advice	3	0.01	advice
140	relationship	19	0.17	relationship, relationships	agreeable	3	0.01	agreeable, enjoy, enjoyable
141	simulation	19	0.16	copied, copy, model, models, simulation, simulations	amount	3	0.01	amount, measures, sum
142	camaraderie	18	0.01	camaraderie	anytime	3	0.03	anytime
143	fun	18	0.09	fun, play, played, playful, playing	argue	3	0.01	argue, indicate, indicated
144	next	18	0.11	follow, followed, following, future, next, succeed	autoscript	3	0.03	autoscript
145	nice	18	0.13	decent, nice, nicely, political, skill, skills	ball	3	0.03	ball, egg, orb
146	share	18	0.13	parcel, part, portion, share, shared, sharing	basic	3	0.02	basic, essential
147	bad	17	0.1	bad, serious, several, sorry	bed	3	0.01	bed, bottom, layers
148	bit	17	0.06	act, bit, turn	begin	3	0.01	begin, begins, sources
149	collaboration	17	0.15	collaborate, collaborating, collaboration, collaborative, cooperation, cooperative	buffer	3	0.02	buffer, pilot
150	group	17	0.14	group, groups, sorts	bump	3	0.01	break, bump
151	minutes	17	0.09	hour, hours, min, minute, minutes	campus	3	0.03	campus
152	several	17	0.06	break, dangerous, individual, individuals, respect, separate, serious, several, single, various	catch	3	0.01	catch, stopped, transmission
153	words	17	0.15	discuss, discussed, discussion, language, word, words	challenging	3	0.03	challenge, challenging
154	closed	16	0.05	close, closed, end, ended, familiar, familiarity, final, fold, intimate, nearly, secrets	channel	3	0.01	channel, channels, transferring
155	questions	16	0.06	head, inquiry, question, questions, wonder, wonderful	commitments	3	0.01	commitments, committed, pull
156	sure	16	0.08	author, certain, sure	concerns	3	0.01	concerns, implications, worries
157	touch	16	0.04	concerns, disturbed, equally, move, moving, relate, relates, relatively, touch	conference	3	0.03	conference
158	call	15	0.06	anticipated, call, called, telephone, visit, visiting	constructivism	3	0.01	constructivisim
159	care	15	0.06	attentive, care, concerns, fear, handle, management, measures, tend, worries	contains	3	0.01	contains, incorporate, incorporating
160	connected	15	0.07	connected, connection, continue, continued, joining, link, relate, relates, relatively, units	coordinated	3	0.01	coordinated, organization, organize
161	dont	15	0.13	dont, dont'	couple	3	0.02	couple, joining, link
162	friend	15	0.09	friend, friendly, friends, support, supporter	culture	3	0.01	culture, political
163	inhibition	15	0.01	Inhibition	curve	3	0.03	curve, curves
164	range	15	0.08	order, place, range, run	damage	3	0.02	damage, wrong
165	send	15	0.05	air, commitments, committed,	defense	3	0.03	defense

				direct, direction, post, posted, send, sending				
166	teacher	15	0.13	instructors, teacher, teachers	digital	3	0.01	digital
167	themes	15	0.04	based, paper, reported, subject, subjective, subjects, themes	disk	3	0.03	disc, disk
168	com	14	0.13	Com	dissertation	3	0.03	dissertation
169	conduct	14	0.05	behavior, carry, channel, channels, conduct, conducting, direct, direction, leading	disturbed	3	0.01	disturbed, troubled, worries
170	people	14	0.13	People	doesn't	3	0.03	Doesn't
171	results	14	0.05	answer, attend, attended, attending, consequence, leading, results	eager	3	0.02	eager, forward, ready
172	also	13	0.12	Also	enable	3	0.03	enable
173	bandwidth	13	0.12	Bandwidth	enough	3	0.02	decent, enough
174	delivered	13	0.03	delivered, having, render, rendering, return, save, saved	etc.	3	0.03	etc.
175	direction	13	0.03	candor, center, centered, direct, direction, focus, guide, management, organization, organize	excellent	3	0.03	excellent
176	free	13	0.12	free, unblock	explains	3	0.03	explain, explains
177	however	13	0.08	however, still, yet	far	3	0.02	far, remote
178	interaction	13	0.12	interact, interacting, interaction, interactions, interactive, interactivity	fascinating	3	0.02	catch, fascinating
179	limited	13	0.04	express, expressed, expression, expressions, limited, limits, special	felt	3	0.03	felt
180	mind	13	0.05	brain, head, listen, mind, minded	flying	3	0.01	flying, pilot, quickly
181	order	13	0.04	consistent, consists, neat, order, put, regular, regularly	foster	3	0.03	foster, fosters
182	provide	13	0.04	allow, allowed, allows, provide, providing, render, rendering	guide	3	0.01	guide, run
183	reconnectin g	13	0.01	reconnecting	hollow	3	0.02	empty, hollow
184	system	13	0.08	order, organization, organize, system, systems	hypothesis	3	0.01	guess, hypothesis
185	type	13	0.09	case, cases, type, typed, types	immediately	3	0.01	immediately, prompt, quickly
186	viewer	13	0.12	Viewer	immigrants	3	0.01	immigrants
187	access	12	0.04	access, addition, approach, approaches, available	indeed	3	0.03	indeed
188	air	12	0.05	air, barely, breeze, line, public, publication, spread, vent	intelligent	3	0.01	intelligent
189	assignments	12	0.04	assign, assignments, design, parcel, portion, put, transferring	joining	3	0.01	joining, sum, units
190	choose	12	0.05	choose, prefer, preferable, preferences	joyous	3	0.01	joyous
191	clear	12	0.05	author, clarity, clear, clearly,	levity	3	0.01	levity

				light, lighting, lights				
192	committee	12	0.01	committee	material	3	0.01	material, materials, stuff
193	cool	12	0.11	cold, cool	met	3	0.03	met
194	difficult	12	0.08	difficult, difficulty, hard	misunderstandi ngs	3	0.01	misunderstandings
195	distance	12	0.07	distance, space, spaces	night	3	0.03	night
196	firestorm	12	0.11	#firestorm, firestorm	nothing	3	0.03	nothing, zero
197	identify	12	0.02	identity, individual, individuals	obligation	3	0.01	obligation, responses, responsibilities
198	island	12	0.11	island	opportunities	3	0.03	opportunities, opportunity
199	lot	12	0.06	loaded, lot, luck, portion, ton	owned	3	0.02	having, owned
200	members	12	0.11	member, members	prim	3	0.03	prim, prims
201	pretty	12	0.06	middle, moderate, moderator, pretty, reason, reasons	profession	3	0.01	profession
202	accomplish	11	0.03	accomplish, acquisition, management, realize, skill, skills	professional	3	0.03	pro, professional
203	back	11	0.02	back, support, supporter	protected	3	0.01	protected, protection, secure
204	case	11	0.03	case, cases, events, showcase, subject, subjective, subjects	quality	3	0.01	calibration, quality
205	change	11	0.09	change, changed, changes, exchange, transferring, varies	questionnaire	3	0.03	questionnaire
206	communicat ion	11	0.09	communicate, communication, community, nation	quite	3	0.01	quite, rather, stopped
207	done	11	0.1	done	room	3	0.01	board, room
208	expectation s	11	0.03	anticipated, ask, carry, expect, expectations, require, required, requires	site	3	0.02	site, website
209	found	11	0.04	creation, found, foundation, initially, initiate, innovative, introduction	slow	3	0.01	behind, slow
210	given	11	0.06	given, mind, minded, tend	sorts	3	0.01	screen, sorts
211	happy	11	0.1	glad, happiness, happy	sun	3	0.03	sun
212	hard	11	0.04	hard, heavily, heavy, several, strong	time zones	3	0.01	time zones
213	narrative	11	0.05	narrative, stories, story	trustworthiness	3	0.01	trustworthiness
214	office	11	0.04	author, functioning, functions, office, part, roles	typical	3	0.03	typical
215	preferable	11	0.05	orient, oriented, prefer, preferable, preferences, rather	upper	3	0.02	speed, upper
216	robe	11	0.09	cloth, clothes, robe, robe', robes	willing	3	0.03	willing
217	saved	11	0.07	protected, protection, save, saved, write, writing, writings	win	3	0.01	succeed, win
218	thought	11	0.04	attentive, consideration, contemplated, opinion, opinions, reflection, thought, thoughts, view	absolutely	2	0.02	absolutely
219	vicarious	11	0.01	vicarious	adapt	2	0.02	adapt, version
220	add	10	0.05	add, bring, bringing, brings,	advocate	2	0.02	advocate, counselors

				lends, sum				
221	adjust	10	0.03	adapt, adjust, adjusting, allow, allowed, allows, familiar, familiarity, fit	ago	2	0.02	ago
222	always	10	0.09	always, constant, ever	angry	2	0.02	angry
223	busy	10	0.04	busy, concerns, engaged, engagement, job, line	animated	2	0.02	animated, flesh
224	follow	10	0.02	follow, followed, following, succeed, watch, watching	animotos	2	0.02	animotos
225	form	10	0.02	form, kind, organization, organize, shape, shapes, sorts, spring	asberger	2	0.02	asberger
226	friendship	10	0.09	friendship, friendships	asynchronous	2	0.01	asynchronous
227	hello	10	0.09	hello	Attentive	2	0.02	attentive, regarding
228	instructions	10	0.02	command, direct, direction, instructions	Behind	2	0.02	behind, bottom
229	intercom	10	0.09	intercom	Blog	2	0.01	blog
230	little	10	0.08	little, small	Blue	2	0.02	blue, gentle
231	love	10	0.04	dear, enjoy, enjoyable, love, loved	Board	2	0.02	board, card
232	notes	10	0.05	line, mark, mentioned, note, notes, notice	Bothered	2	0.02	bothered, troubled
233	research	10	0.08	exploring, inquiry, research	Brother	2	0.02	brother
234	right	10	0.04	correctly, decent, proper, properly, right, truly	cautionary	2	0.01	cautionary
235	sense	10	0.04	perceive, sense	Choppy	2	0.02	choppy
236	story	10	0.04	levels, reported, stories, story	Christmas	2	0.02	Christmas
237	subject	10	0.02	dependency, depends, matter, nation, subject, subjective, subjects, submit	College	2	0.02	college
238	support	10	0.03	document, encouragement, support, supporter	Colors	2	0.02	colors
239	survey	10	0.03	follow, followed, following, survey, view	complaints	2	0.01	complaints
240	things	10	0.08	matter, thing, things	conducive	2	0.02	conducive, leading
241	together	10	0.08	together, units	conferencing	2	0.01	conferencing
242	active	9	0.06	active, activities, activity, dynamic, dynamically	Congrats	2	0.02	congrats
243	among	9	0.08	among	consequence	2	0.02	consequence, therefore
244	classroom	9	0.08	classroom	consideration	2	0.02	consideration, retainable
245	common	9	0.08	common, mutually, normal, usually	cost	2	0.02	cost, dear
246	curriculum	9	0.04	curriculum, program, programs	courage	2	0.01	courage
247	definitely	9	0.08	decided, definitely, definition	crucial	2	0.02	crucial, essential
248	easy	9	0.04	easy, gentle, light, lighting, lights, slow, slowly	deception	2	0.01	deception
249	express	9	0.02	carry, express, expressed, expression, expressions, reflection, verbal	decided	2	0.02	decided, resolve
250	graphics	9	0.08	art, graphic, graphics	decrease	2	0.02	decrease, decreased

251	intimate	9	0.02	familiar, familiarity, inner, intimate, knowledge, suggest, suggested, suggestions	default	2	0.02	default
252	inventory	9	0.08	inventory, 'inventory	demonstrate	2	0.02	demonstrate, evident
253	live	9	0.03	animated, live, lives, merry	difficulty	2	0.02	difficulty, troubled
254	others	9	0.07	early, others, separate	dimension	2	0.02	dimension, properties
255	redirect	9	0.01	redirect	Disney	2	0.02	Disney
256	sent	9	0.08	sent	domain	2	0.02	domain, land
257	sometimes	9	0.06	old, sometimes	due	2	0.02	due
258	success	9	0.07	consecutive, succeed, success, successful, successfully	empty	2	0.02	empty, vacations
259	understood	9	0.01	understood	ethics	2	0.01	ethics
260	years	9	0.04	day, year, years	evaluate	2	0.02	evaluate, measures
261	ability	8	0.05	abilities, ability	every time	2	0.01	every time
262	act	8	0.02	act, move, moving	everywhere	2	0.02	everywhere
263	around	8	0.07	around	exchange	2	0.02	exchange, substitute
264	attend	8	0.02	attend, attended, attending, attentive, hang, listen, serve	experiential	2	0.01	experiential
265	built	8	0.07	built	experts	2	0.02	experts, technical
266	Colorado	8	0.07	Colorado	fabulous	2	0.02	fabulous, fantastic
267	command	8	0.02	command, control, require, required, requires	facial	2	0.02	facial
268	compare	8	0.03	compare, comparison, relate, relates, relatively	fascinating	2	0.01	fascinating
269	content	8	0.02	argue, content, subject, subjective, subjects	fallen	2	0.02	fallen
270	holidays	8	0.07	holiday, holidays, vacations	fancy	2	0.02	fancy, notion
271	instance	8	0.03	immediately, instance, instances	filtering	2	0.02	filtering
272	low	8	0.03	blue, low, small	flash	2	0.02	flash, instantly
273	maps	8	0.06	functioning, functions, mapped, mapping, maps	folder	2	0.02	folder
274	offline	8	0.07	offline	freedom	2	0.02	freedom
275	phenomeno n	8	0.01	phenomenon	from	2	0.02	from
276	physical	8	0.05	animated, material, materials, physical, physically	frustrating	2	0.01	frustrating
277	platform	8	0.05	platform, program, programs	geographically	2	0.02	geographically, geography
278	positive	8	0.03	advantage, perspective, positive, status, submit, view	gifts	2	0.02	gifts, talents
279	potential	8	0.02	capabilities, potential	glorious	2	0.01	glorious
280	problem	8	0.06	job, problem, problems, troubled	haha	2	0.02	haha
281	reasons	8	0.02	argue, reason, reasons, sound, sounds	hang	2	0.02	hang, knack
282	refocus	8	0.01	refocus	harder	2	0.02	harder
283	request	8	0.07	ask, quest, request, requested	hardware	2	0.02	hardware
284	select	8	0.04	quality, select, selecting, selection	heard	2	0.02	heard

285	sim	8	0.07	sim, sims	hey	2	0.02	hey
286	turn	8	0.02	becomes, becoming, off', turn	hud	2	0.02	hud
287	wonderful	8	0.04	fantastic, terrific, wonder, wonderful	imposters	2	0.02	imposters
288	accept	7	0.03	accept, accepted, recognize, recognized	inception	2	0.01	inception
289	addition	7	0.03	addition, improvement, improving, increase, increased, increases, increasing	industry	2	0.02	industry
290	answer	7	0.03	answer, resolve, responses, responsibilities, serve	inner	2	0.02	inner, inside
291	area	7	0.03	area, country, domain, field	innovative	2	0.02	innovative, introduced
292	believe	7	0.04	believe, credibility, plausible, probably	irresistible	2	0.02	irresistible, overwhelming
293	flowing	7	0.03	currently, flowed, flowing, hang, period, stream	journal	2	0.02	journal, journals
294	hear	7	0.02	audience, hear, hearing, listen	jump	2	0.02	jump, spring
295	laugh	7	0.06	laugh, laughed, laughing, laughs	kinesthetic	2	0.01	kinesthetic
296	motivation	7	0.02	motivation, move, moving, prompt	latest	2	0.02	latest
297	never	7	0.06	never	layers	2	0.02	layers, levels
298	part	7	0.02	break, component, components, part, portion, separate	leaders	2	0.02	leaders, leadership
299	remained	7	0.03	continue, continued, remained, rests, stay	leadership	2	0.02	leadership, leading
300	rendering	7	0.01	render, rendering, return, submit, version	learners	2	0.02	learners
301	representati ons	7	0.01	representations	lifted	2	0.02	lifted, vacations
302	required	7	0.02	essential, necessary, require, required, requires	log	2	0.02	Log
303	respect	7	0.03	creditability, esteem, regarding, respect	loss	2	0.02	loss, red
304	signing	7	0.06	gestures, mark, sign, signing	media	2	0.02	media
305	space	7	0.02	separate, space, spaces	microphone	2	0.02	microphone
306	task	7	0.03	job, task, tasks	might	2	0.02	might
307	university	7	0.04	general, universities, university, worldwide	mistakes	2	0.02	mistakes
308	viper	7	0.06	viper	modality	2	0.02	modality, mode
309	without	7	0.06	without	montage	2	0.02	montage
310	actual	6	0.02	actual, actuality, actually, realize	MOOC	2	0.01	MOOC
311	anything	6	0.05	anything	music	2	0.02	music
312	audio	6	0.02	audio, sound, sounds	must	2	0.02	must
313	bring	6	0.01	bring, bringing, brings, land	mybase	2	0.02	mybase
314	chair	6	0.03	chair, leading, moderate, moderator	navigating	2	0.02	navigating, pilot
315	collect	6	0.05	collect, compiling, gather	necessary	2	0.02	necessary
316	comfortable	6	0.03	cheers, comfort, comfortable,	neutral	2	0.01	neutral

				easy				
317	conversational	6	0.02	conversation, conversational, familiar, familiarity	none	2	0.02	none
318	critical	6	0.05	critical, critically, crucial	notecard	2	0.02	notecard, notecard'
319	date	6	0.02	date, engaged, engagement	past	2	0.02	past, spread
320	emerge	6	0.05	emerge, emerged, emerging	product	2	0.02	product, richness
321	especially	6	0.04	especially, exceptional, particular, special	professors	2	0.01	professors
322	everything	6	0.05	everything	propensity	2	0.02	propensity
323	extending	6	0.02	carry, continue, continued, expand, extending	quickly	2	0.02	quickly, ready
324	f2f	6	0.05	f2f	railing	2	0.02	railing, training
325	faculty	6	0.05	faculty	regarding	2	0.02	regarding, wish
326	fine	6	0.05	alright, fine, okay	regardless	2	0.02	regardless
327	graduation	6	0.05	calibration, graduation	reject	2	0.02	reject, resistant
328	guidance	6	0.03	direct, direction, guidance	remote	2	0.02	remote, removed
329	happens	6	0.03	happening, happens, material, materials, occurrences	removed	2	0.02	removed, transferring
330	high	6	0.05	high, richness	restart	2	0.02	restart
331	involved	6	0.01	involved, involves, regarding	rezzer	2	0.02	rezzer
332	item	6	0.02	item, items, list	safe	2	0.02	safe, safety
333	message	6	0.04	content, message, messages	sat	2	0.02	sat
334	network	6	0.04	mesh, network, web	secure	2	0.02	secure, strong
335	paraphrase	6	0.01	paraphrase	seeds	2	0.02	seeds, sources
336	private	6	0.02	individual, individuals, private, secrets	self	2	0.01	self
337	process	6	0.02	process, progression, serve	separate	2	0.01	separate
338	programs	6	0.02	plans, program, programs, scheduling	size	2	0.02	size, sized
339	purpose	6	0.02	design, purpose, resolve	sketchy	2	0.02	sketchy
340	remember	6	0.03	memory, remember	slider	2	0.02	slider
341	resembles	6	0.01	resembles	slurl	2	0.02	slurl
342	script	6	0.04	hand, script, written	Speed	2	0.02	speed, swift
343	since	6	0.05	since	square	2	0.02	square, squares
344	something	6	0.05	something	strange	2	0.02	strange
345	sound	6	0.01	heavy, sound, sounds, wise	taught	2	0.02	taught
346	term	6	0.03	damage, term, terms	teammates	2	0.02	teammates
347	tool	6	0.05	instrument, tool, tools	techniques	2	0.02	techniques
348	track	6	0.02	leading, railing, run, track, trail	teleconference	2	0.02	teleconference
349	vapor	6	0.04	blue, flying, transparent, vapor	terrain	2	0.02	terrain
350	week	6	0.05	week, weeks	therefore	2	0.02	therefore, thus
351	another	5	0.04	another	tomorrow	2	0.01	tomorrow

352	approach	5	0.01	approach, approaches, nearly	Took	2	0.02	took
353	averages	5	0.02	averages, middle, modality	Trail	2	0.02	trail, training
354	based	5	0.02	based, foundation	transdisciplinarity	2	0.01	transdisciplinarity
355	benevolence	5	0.04	benevolence, kind	undergoing	2	0.02	undergoing
356	bond	5	0.04	bond	Vice	2	0.02	vice
357	break	5	0.01	break, check, checked, separate, stopped	willingness	2	0.02	willingness
358	cap	5	0.04	cap, capital	wouldn't	2	0.02	wouldn't
359	check	5	0.01	check, checked, contains, mark, stopped				

APPENDIX E: NVIVO CODING EXAMPLE

For readable version of all the codes go to https://www.dropbox.com/sh/no8415euzoimwdn/vj4p3kp885

APPENDIX F: NVIVO CLUSTER MAP OF WORD SIMILARITY

For readable version of all the codes go to https://www.dropbox.com/sh/no8415euzoimwdn/vj4p3kp885 or scan the QR code above.

TABLES & FIGURES